New England Art Pottery

of the Arts and Crafts Movement

Paul A. Royka

4880 Lower Valley Road, Atglen, PA 19310

DEDICATION

To my wonderful wife, Deborah, who has persevered, sacrificed, and supported my work on this book; to my mother, Margaret, who has always helped me achieve my dreams, and in memory of my father, Robert, who taught me to take my own path.

Royka, Paul A.
    Fireworks : New England art pottery of the arts and crafts movement / Paul A. Royka
        p.   cm.
    Includes bibliographical references.
    ISBN 0-88740-988-1 (hardcover)
    1. Art pottery, American--New England. 2. Art pottery--19th century--New England. 3. Art pottery--20th century--New England. 4. Arts and crafts movement--New England. I. Title.
NK4010.R69 1997
738'.0974'09034--dc21   97-24474
                                            CIP

Published by Schiffer Publishing Ltd.
4880 Lower Valley Road
Atglen, PA 19310
Phone: (610) 593-1777; Fax: (610) 593-2002
E-mail: Schifferbk@aol.com
Please write for a free catalog.
This book may be purchased from the publisher.
Please include $3.95 for shipping.
Try your bookstore first.

We are interested in hearing from authors with book ideas on related subjects.

ISBN: 0-88740-988-1
Printed in Hong Kong
1 2 3 4

Book Design by: Blair R.C. Loughrey

PREFACE

New England art pottery is an exciting field with new information being found every day. There are still exceptional buys to be made, especially in the works of Hugh Robertson, who is still neglected by most collectors.

In general, the prices assigned to items are retail and assume the items are in perfect condition.

Comments or inquiries can be sent to:

Design20c@aol.com or you can visit the author's web site at www.Design20c.com. Mail can be sent to Paul Royka, 210 Park Avenue #295, Worcester, MA 01609.

ACKNOWLEDGEMENTS

I would like to thank Skinner Inc., JMW Gallery, Rod McKenzie, Anthony Leite, and everyone who encouraged me to finish this project. Also, a special thanks to editor Douglas Congdon-Martin at Schiffer Publishing for his patience, and Stanley P. Bystrowski for his photography work, including the cover.

TABLE OF CONTENTS

INTRODUCTION

Defining "Arts and Crafts"

The concept of "arts and crafts" began as early as 1834 with the philosophical writings of several English artists and critics. These ideas were translated into the decorative arts of some of the leading designers of the 1870s. The phrase "arts and crafts" was first coined in 1888 by a student at the Royal Academy in London as an alternative to the phrase "fine arts," which spoke of only paintings and sculpture, relegating decorative arts to a second class. As the Arts and Crafts Movement developed, it became more associated with a loosely connected set of ideas rather than any specific style or social policy. The attitude of an object's creator had more to do with describing an item as "arts and crafts" than the object itself.

Philosophical Beginnings

England's artistic intelligentsia had the greatest influence on artisans in the United States. An avant garde artistic challenge in the mid-nineteenth century known as the Pre-Raphaelite movement was the germ that would radically change decorative arts. In 1848, a group of artists including William Holman Hunt, John Everett Millias, and Dante Gabriel Rossetti joined to create an English school of painting genuinely based on nature. At the time, the Royal Academy's Schools used rigorous technical instruction intended to create a pattern of formal ideas based upon a system of reference to classical literature and mythology. The Pre-Raphaelite artists became known as The Brotherhood and they emphasized a philosophy that the post-Renaissance style was detrimental to the world of art.

The two strongest voices for this view, besides the artists themselves, were August Welby Northmore Pugin (1812-1852) and John Ruskin (1819-1900). In 1834, Pugin published *Contrasts,* a work in which he discussed the connection between architecture and life. He wrote of the purity of medieval cathedrals and rural life and the visual and spiritual ugliness of the industrial age. His works contributed to the revival of the Gothic school of architects and the behaviorist view of architecture prevalent in American architects such as Frank Lloyd Wright.

John Ruskin, Slade Professor of Art at Oxford University, was the most influential of all Victorian writers on

the arts. He vigorously attacked the view of the Royal Academy's School in support of post-Renaissance style. For him the concept of a "school of design" was impossible. He felt that drawing might be taught by teachers, but design could only be taught by Nature. *The Stones of Venice* was published in 1853 and had a profound influence on both sides of the Atlantic. His views would influence every artisan in the United States:

> *"Men were not intended to work with the accuracy of tools, to be precise and perfect in all their actions. If you will have that precision out of them you must unhumanise them.*
>
> *If you will make a man of the working creature you cannot make a tool. Let him but begin to imagine, to think, to try to do anything worth doing, and ... out come all his roughness, all his incapacity ... failure after failure ... but out comes the whole majesty of him also."*
>
> *"We want one man to be always thinking, and another to be always working, and we call one man a gentleman, and the other an operative; whereas the workman ought often to be thinking, and the thinker often to be working, and both should be gentlemen, in the best sense.... It would be well if all of us were good handicraftsmen in some kind, and the dishonor of manual labor done away with altogether. [We see] the degradation of the operative into machine.... It is not that men are ill fed, but that they have no pleasure in the work by which they make their bread and therefor look to wealth as the only means of pleasure."*

Ruskin's writings became available to the American art community in 1851 when John Wiley published Ruskin's Pre-Raphaelite pamphlet in New York. In 1857, Pre-Raphaelitism in America was stimulated by the exhibition of contemporary British art in New York. The exhibition traveled to Boston with 356 objects. The British artist Rossetti was a key figure in bringing this exhibition about. Two magazines, *The Crayon* and *The New Path* would disseminate Ruskin's ideas to the general public in America. The fundamental importance of Ruskin's writing in America was his ability to connect art with morality and religion through an exploration of nature. This struck a response from the American public which already held an attitude of reverence for nature.

This response created the American Pre-Raphaelites. A group of artists during the 1850s and 1860s opposed the teachings of the National Academy in New York and the Pennsylvania Academy of Fine Arts because their views were similar to the Royal Academy's School in London. American Pre-Raphaelites believed that a study of nature should be completed outdoors. They opposed the Hudson River School of artists who would make sketches in pen and pencil in natural surroundings but compose their paintings in studios. The American Pre-Raphaelites believed this style of painting was untrue to nature. American Pre-Raphaelites practiced painting with a heightened meticulousness and specificity of detail that was good enough for a botanist. This was referred to as the Ruskinian lens. The artists removes himself from the work to allow nature to speak for itself.

In America, Charles Eliot Norton became the direct link for spreading Ruskin's philosophy to New England. A friend of John Ruskin, he was appointed Professor of the History of Art at Harvard University in 1875 and continued this position for twenty-three years. It should be noted that this was the first position of its kind in the United States. It was only in 1867 that John Stuart Mill, as rector of the University of St. Andrews, suggested that culture in the arts be admitted as an essential portion of education. From this position, Norton was able to influence the views of the artistic intelligentsia in New England.

Philosophy Becomes Decorative Arts

As a student at Oxford University, William Morris (1834-1896) was strongly influenced by Ruskin's teachings. In 1857, at the age of 23, he collaborated in the painting of Pre-Raphaelite frescoes in the Oxford Union. By 1861, at the age of 27, Morris became the first artist to successfully incorporate the ideas of the Pre-Raphaelites into the decorative arts. He founded Morris, Marshall, Faulkner, and Company, which later became Morris and Company in 1875, and produced all types of interior furnishings including stained glass, wallpapers, fabrics, and furniture. He even went as far as incorporating Pre-Raphaelite paintings into the doors of some of his furniture. These objects were in opposition to those made upon classical references. Victorian design elements of the post Renaissance incorporated an eclectic mix of Greek, Roman, and Italian Renaissance styles produced cheaply by the new machinery of the industrial revolution. Morris's concerns were a mix of aesthetic and social reform. He believed he could improve a worker's life if the worker cared about what he produced and therefore found satisfaction and pleasure in his work.

Another major English design reformer was Charles Locke Eastlake. He was the author of *Hints on Household Taste* in 1868. This book expressed the principles of simplicity, functionalism, and honesty of construction. His furniture designs were marked by a lightness unseen in Renaissance and Gothic revival forms; veneers were scorned in favor of hand construction. Eastlake admired the way in which simple medieval furniture was made by hand rather than the imitation of specific styles from the past eras, thereby freeing his followers from strict adherence to historical motifs.

Arthur Lasenby Liberty (1843-1917) was the founder of Liberty & Company. The company specialized in the production of textiles and interior furnishings in the Art Nouveau style (characterized by organic, undulating lines) which would become known as "Stile Liberty." After a trip to Japan in 1889, he began incorporating Japanese themes into his furnishings. Liberty employed some of the most important designers of the period including Christopher Dresser, C.F.A. Voysey, and Archibald Knox.

Oriental Influences

Exhibitions during the 1860s and 1870s ignited a taste for the Japanese aesthetic. The London International Exhibition in 1862 placed on display objects collected by Sir Rutherford Alcock, British prime minister to Japan. These objects helped spur later appetites for Liberty & Company's products. In 1867, the Exposition Universelle in Paris would inspire potters to create objects in the Japanese style. The Centennial Exposition of 1876 in Philadelphia provided the general American public with its first view of the new style and the English and Continental potteries adaptation of these new ideas. The simplicity of Oriental design was easily associated with the simplified style of Ruskin and Morris.

Arts and Crafts Movement in New England

During the latter part of the nineteenth century, New England's industrial centers were attracting hundreds of thousands of European immigrants. The elite hierarchy of existing political and social institutions felt threatened. The Brahmin society of Boston, composed of the Protestant elite, founded the Immigration Restriction League in 1894. But needing labor to feed the growing industrial empires required these anti-immigration proponents to change their agenda to create "Americanization" programs to assimilate the new immigrants. The popularity of John Ruskin's philosophy which combined social and artistic aims appealed to the supporters of the Americanization process. The striking incongruity of teaching arts to European immigrants who had excelled in these skills for centuries never occurred to the elite.

A premier cultural institution founded upon these ideals was the Museum of Fine Arts in Boston, founded on July 4, 1876. The museum not only exhibited objects to inspire the local public but also opened a museum school to put these concepts into practice. The appeal for art education had been acted upon as early as 1870 when general art education was legislated in Massachusetts schools.

Boston would be the site of the first arts and crafts exhibition society, known as the Boston Society of Arts and Crafts, in the United States. Charles Eliot Norton (a friend of Ruskin's) would become its first president. The organization resembled the Arts and Crafts Exhibition Society of London. A venue was created in which artists could submit their objects for display, be critiqued by judges and find business opportunities with potential clients. The New England museums were actively supportive of the artists, purchasing items for their museum collections and holding exhibitions of their works. Members of the society lived throughout New England and later artists throughout the United States would submit objects for review, hoping to be recognized. Most New England potters used the society both to exhibit and to be inspired by others. The society became the model for hundreds of exhibition societies throughout the country and remains in business today, exhibiting the works of contemporary artists.

Evaluating Art Pottery

In order to evaluate an item of art pottery, we must be able to identify it first. Debate usually exists around any phrase that contains the word "art." Art pottery is no different. Art historians, dealers and collectors have continually tried to define this phrase to explain their inclusion or exclusion of certain pottery. One of the most comprehensive definitions was devised by Paul Evans, author of *Art Pottery of the United States* (1974). He stated:

> "Art pottery, then, is not identified by particular styles or techniques, specific operations or span of years, but rather by the philosophy or attitude of the individuals involved in its execution. The term itself defines the product of creative tension between artistic and technical skills within a commercial organization. When combined with the productive techniques of the age, this union resulted in the output of art objects which bear witness to the unique talents of those involved in their execution."

Evans definition also allowed him to distinguish between art pottery and what he called industrial artware and studio pottery. Industrial artware is to be understood as something created to look like handicraft but executed by a mechanized process capable of reproducing the object in mass. Studio pottery is the opposite—the object is the creation of one artist, is produced in a studio, and is relatively unique. More or less this has been the standard by which most collectors decide if an item falls into the category of art pottery.

Now that we are closer to understanding what an item of art pottery is, we need to know how to distinguish between the average or exceptional item. Most collectors of art pottery use subjective phrases to explain their appreciation of items they have or want to buy. This is sometimes referred to as "object speak." A person is heard saying "It speaks to me," "It has a wonderful feel about it," or "It has a wonderful presence." In these cases the collector places their own attitudes and opinions on the piece but do not say anything that distinguishes the value of the item aside from themselves. The philosopher David Hume described this as the "pathetic fallacy." He described this as the mind's propensity to spread itself on the object before it. It may provide the reason why someone is buying an object, but it does not explain why the object itself has value.

Two types of evaluations can be employed to estimate the value of a piece of art pottery. These are called technical and status evaluations. Technical evaluations refer to those that deal with techniques used in the production of an item, such as the history of the maker, form of the item, the clay used, decoration, and how these interrelate. Status evaluation refers to how well an item expresses the ideals for which it was made. Take for example an early piece of Marblehead Pottery (see Chapter 9). Technical evaluations would include how even the glaze is, whether the item is decorated, whether the decoration is in harmony with the form, etc. A status evaluation is that Marblehead Pottery was one of the first to use art pottery as a form of occupational therapy. Its forms were simple and decorated with soft-matte glazes emphasizing the colors of the natural surroundings. Marblehead Pottery expressed ingenuity in design and provided social benefits to its creators. A value is placed not simply upon its technical merit or its decorative appeal, but also its status in relation to the ideals of the Arts and Crafts Movement. One would want to place a higher value on this piece in comparison to a piece of industrial artware, such as Roseville Pottery, which was massed produced, not for the benefit of an individual or ideal, but simply for profit.

Chapter 1

CHELSEA KERAMIC ART WORKS
(1872-1889)

Rare dragon's blood vase, c.1888, $10,000-15,000. *(Skinner Inc.)*

One of the most important contributions to New England art pottery was made by the Robertson family of Chelsea, Massachusetts. The family consisted of the brothers Alexander W., Hugh C., George W. and their father, James. James was born in Edinburgh into a family of potters. He brought his family to the United States in 1853 and worked in the pottery companies of the New Jersey area until 1859. Later that year he moved to East Boston and worked for New England Pottery Company and Plymton & Robertson Pottery until he retired in 1872. Following the family tradition he taught each of his sons the art of pottery making.

His son, Alexander, would be the first to start a small pottery in an abandoned varnish factory in Chelsea, Massachusetts. The nearby clay was suitable for making redware. Redware is a smooth, porous red clay that could be made into utilitarian shapes and decorated by painting. At the age of twenty-two, his brother Hugh joined Alexander and the firm became known as A.W. & H.C. Robertson. Pottery forms at this time had simple decorations with incised designs reminiscent of Victorian silver chasing. When their father joined in 1872, the firm became known as Chelsea Keramic Art Works, Robertson & Sons.

From 1872 to 1876, their products were based upon ancient Greek terra-cotta ceramics. Decoration consisted of simple, un-glazed redware featuring Greek forms with encaustic red or black painting and vases or tiles with impressed natural flowers and geometric designs. By 1878, due to the lack of public support, all redware production was discontinued.

The redware would be replaced following experiments by Hugh Robertson. Hugh had attended the Centennial Exposition at Philadelphia in 1876. He was intrigued by the French underglaze slip-decorated wares and inspired by the colorful glazes of the oriental pottery. Within a year of his return from the exhibition, Chelsea Keramic Art Works introduced a creamware that took colored glazes. Robertson also reproduced the French wares he had seen, calling his line Bourg-la-Reine, after the town that created it. His brother, George, left the company in 1878. His father, James, died in 1880 and his brother, Alexander, left for California in 1884, leaving Hugh in charge. Hugh's experiments would produce the most important efforts of Chelsea Keramic Art Works.

Chelsea Keramic Art Works impressed mark.

Dragon's blood vase with deep red glaze, $5,000-7,000. *(JMW Gallery)*

Dragon's blood vase in gourd form, $2,000. *(JMW Gallery)*

Hugh was most profoundly influenced by the oriental ceramics at the exhibition. He saw the red of Ming porcelain known as dragon's blood (also known as *sang du boeuf* in Europe). He dedicated his career to finding the secret of this glaze. Red had always been the most desired color for ceramic workers. Most potters throughout the world could only produce a light shade of red that seemed superficial at best. Hugh's experiments to reproduce this color created other colors such as deep sea-green, apple-green, mustard-yellow, and turquoise. He also discovered a Japanese crackle glaze that he would use later in his career. It is believed that he first obtained a true dragon's blood glaze in 1885 and perfected it in 1888.

Hugh spent more than ten years perfecting the glaze. He worked day and night in his pottery, grinding the pigment and watching the kiln. He claimed two small vases as his very best red; these became known as the "Twin Stars of Chelsea." They

Same vase showing speckled glaze.

Two Chelsea Keramic Art Works vases each exhibiting a dragon's blood glaze, $2,000 each.

Dragon's blood vase, impressed CKAW, ht.10 ¾", $10,000. (*Collection of Anthony Leite*)

exhibit a deep red glaze highlighted with an iridescent glow. Hugh believed that only about a dozen of these vases were his best. His works were acclaimed in Paris and received prizes at the San Francisco World's Fair and various exhibitions including those held by the Boston Society of Arts and Crafts. The price for all his efforts was public acclaim and financial ruin. In 1889, the company closed due to financial difficulties.

The works of Chelsea Keramic Art Works are prized among serious pottery collectors who appreciate the amount of effort that went into them. Early works done in the Greek style are very rare. The dragon's blood vases and other finely glazed items in the Oriental tradition are the most sought after and command the highest prices. One of the earliest marks has the words "Chelsea Keramic Art Works" above "Robertson & Sons." The impressed mark "CKAW" was used from 1875 until 1889. For the most part, only Robertson family members designed and signed the ware. Pieces would be signed with incised initials of the artist usually found in the decoration itself. Decorators included Hugh Robertson, Alexander Robertson, Josephine Day, G.W. Fenety, and Franz Dengler.

Vase exhibiting dark red glaze, 6", $1,200.

Dragon's blood vase, 3 ¼", $500-700.

Vase exhibiting porous glaze,
5 ½", $1,200. (*JMW Gallery*)

14

Dripping dragon's blood glaze on a dark background, impressed CKAW, ht. 7 ½", $6,000. (*Collection of Anthony Leite*)

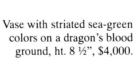

Vase with striated sea-green colors on a dragon's blood ground, ht. 8 ½", $4,000.

Opposite page:
Dragon's blood vase exhibiting a vibrant, mottled iridescent glaze, ht. 8 ½", $6,000. (*Skinner Inc.*)

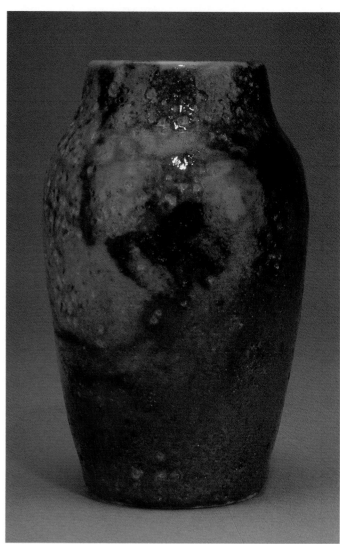

Vase with dark, mottled glaze, impressed CKAW, ht. 8", $2,500.

Chelsea Keramic Art Works vase exhibiting a variety of colors, ht.7 ¾", $3,000. (*JMW Gallery*)

Vase with dark glaze, $1,000.

16

Chelsea Keramic Art Works bowl with
striated glaze, diameter 8", $500.

Chelsea Keramic Art Works vase
with sea-green glaze, ht.4", $300.

Unusual CKAW vase displaying a dripping
glaze with flower-like forms, $2,500.

Unusual CKAW vase with a Chinese-style white background, ht. 8 ½", $5,000. (Skinner Inc.)

Exceptional Chelsea Keramic Art Works tile with electroplated copper, signed by Hugh Robertson, $10,000.

Chapter 2

CHELSEA POTTERY U.S. & DEDHAM POTTERY
(1891-1894)   (1895-1943)

Early C.P.U.S. plate with rabbit-pattern facing left.

Plate decorated by Maud Davenport. Notice the small circle on the leaf in the lower right hand corner.

Plate decorated by Charles Davenport. Notice the baby elephant on the top right hand corner.

Hugh Robertson's achievements were well known in Boston public after he exhibited in the first Boston Society of Arts and Crafts exhibition in 1897. After Chelsea Keramic Art Works closed in 1889, a group of Bostonians supplied funds to form a company and reopen the pottery with Hugh Robertson as superintendent. Among the benefactors of the new Chelsea Pottery, USA were Arthur Astor Carey as president, Horace D. Chapin as treasurer, and directors: A. Wadsworth Longfellow, Jr., J. Templeman Coolidge, Jr., R. Clipston Sturgis, Joseph Linden Smith, Sara W. Whitman, and William Sturgis Bigelow. Another Boston Society of Arts and Crafts member, Charles Mills, was the director of decorating. Hugh's son, William, took charge of firing the pottery.

As a condition of financial support, the benefactors convinced Hugh to produce a line of art pottery for the general public. Hugh incorporated a crackle glaze that he discovered while working on the dragon's blood glaze with a cobalt rabbit design by Charles Mills. The decoration consisted of a repeated rabbit design in a circular border. For the first year the rabbit pattern faced left but was changed to the right after 1891 to make it easier for the right handed decorators. The Museum of Fine Arts School, Boston, helped to secure new designs by students through competitions in which the best design would be utilized by the pottery company.

The dampness in the area created problems in firing the new crackleware and a search was undertaken to move the pottery to a more suitable location. Dedham, Massachusetts proved to be the best site and construction for the new plant began in 1893. Operations transferred in the latter part of 1894 and production started in 1895. At that time the name was changed to Dedham Pottery.

Dedham Pottery's crackleware was a great commercial success. More than fifty different patterns were incorporated on a wide variety of forms. The making of the ware consisted of bringing together a host of raw materials. Clay from Kentucky, English china clay, German cobalt, and gold for Hugh's Dragon Blood glaze. The crackleware plates were made between hinged molds with raised designs on a rotating jigger wheel. As the artists' freehand decoration improved the raised designs were no longer needed.

The secret of the crackle glaze was recounted in *The Dedham Pottery* by Dr. Lloyd E. Hawes:

"[Mr. Davenport] relates that the secret process occurred after the second or 'gloss' firing, which took 24 hours. The blue decorated pieces, still very warm from the 'gloss' kiln, were hauled up to the garret of the main building by a hand operated, rope-pulled elevator. As the cool air off the elevator shaft struck the warm glaze, a very audible crackling could be heard. The elevator was rushed past the showroom floor, so that this sound would not reach the customers. At times, the elevator would decide to slip downwards of its own volition, and only a quick transfer of hands to brake rope would forestay disaster."

After the pottery was removed from the elevator it was cooled and rubbed with a black substance that would enhance the presence of the crackle. Sometimes the white glaze was tinted to a gray, pink, or green. Recently a plate was discovered with its original sticker referring to the experimental glaze as "Smokey Cracqule."

Dedham Pottery vase
showing Hugh
Robertson's lava-style
glaze. *Courtesy of
Anthony Leite.*

Bottom of lava vase incised
Dedham Pottery and initials
for Hugh C. Robertson.

Two of the most prominent decorators were Maude Davenport and her brother, Charles. Maude started with the company in 1904. Her work is easily distinguished from the other decorators. Her work is detailed and elegant. A pattern such as Magnolia became crisp in her hands, exhibiting detail through care and talent. Her work is usually signed with a small blue circle in the pattern of a piece. She resigned in 1929.

Her brother, Charles, began decorating in 1914. His most memorable contribution is the Elephant pattern. It was designed for the Republican Party at the time of President Teddy Roosevelt. The baby elephant was incorporated in the design to fix an accident in the spacing of the pattern. Charles is also credited with modeling items in wet clay such as the small frog paperweights.

While the company enjoyed the success of the crackle ware, Hugh was able to resume his experiments. Vessels produced at this time used heavy flowing glazes that look like lava flowing from a volcano. The forms remained Oriental in flavor and were signed Dedham Pottery along with Hugh's initials HCR. On May 26, 1908, possibly due to lead poisoning from the glazes, Hugh Robertson died.

His son, William, continued the family tradition. William had been hurt in a kiln accident in 1904 which prevented him from modeling the clay. Dedham pottery would rely upon the designs of his father for the rest of its existence. Raw materials became increasingly difficult to secure during the first World War and the quality of the pottery suffered. William would die on January 17, 1929.

J. Milton Robertson, William's son, continued on as the seventh generation of his family to make pottery. At this time, the company began to place the word "Registered" under its blue stamp mark. A catalogue of wares was created in 1938 which distinguished between "Regular" and "Special" patterns:

Regular patterns included the rabbit, clover, turkey, polar bear, azalea, duck, grape, horse chestnut, magnolia, snow tree, butterfly, iris, and water lily designs. Special patterns included the elephant, lion, crab, bird in orange tree, swan, lobster, dolphin, chicken, turtle, and owl designs.

J. Milton accepted a commission as a commander in the United States Navy and decided to close the pottery. The operation ceased operation on April 17, 1943.

Gimbles Department Store in New York City liquidated the inventory of Dedham Pottery. The prices reflected the importance of the items. Hugh's Dragon Blood vases were advertised for $250, six weeks pay for the average worker. A Gimbels' advertisement stated:

"Its makers were much more interested in technical and artistic problems than in selling ... No other potters in the world have ever found the secret of the Ming sang-de-boeuf or the spider-web fine crackle of priceless Ming porcelains."

Dedham Pottery rabbit stamp.

Dedham Pottery rabbit stamp with registered mark.

Dedham Historical Society Exhibition sticker from 1968.

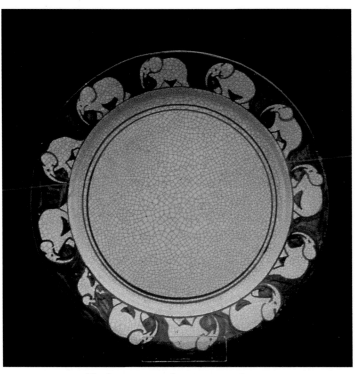

Elephant-pattern plate, stamp and
impressed rabbit, 8 ¼", $600. (*Skinner*)

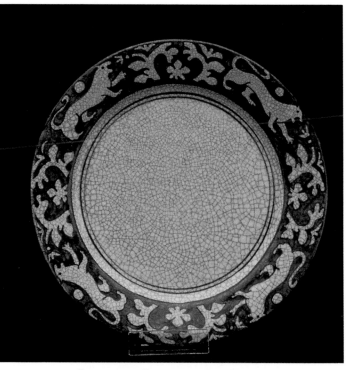

Rare tapestry lion-pattern plate, stamp
and impressed rabbit, 8 ½", $1,100.

Duck-pattern plates, stamp and impressed rabbits, 8 ½", $300 each.

Butterfly pattern plates, stamp and impressed rabbit, 6", $400 each.

Pond lily plates, blue stamp and impressed rabbit, 6", $200 each.

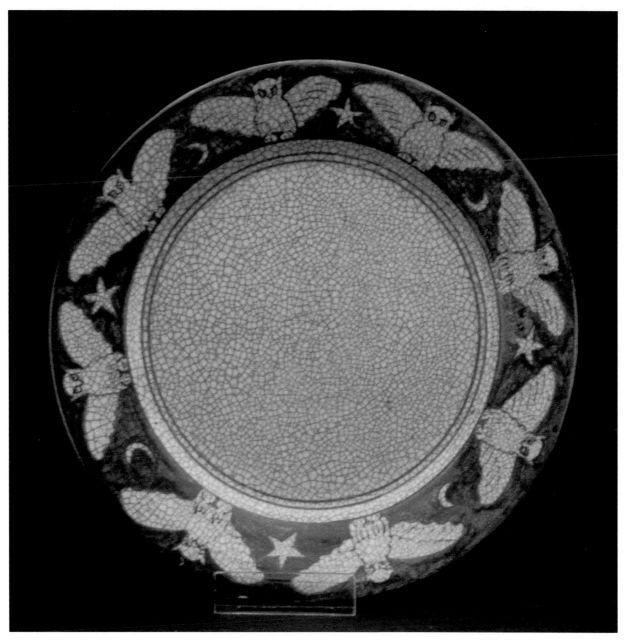

Rare owl-pattern plate with woman's face, blue
stamp and star mark, 8 ½", $3,000. (*Skinner*)

If you look closely you
can see a face looking
out beneath the star.

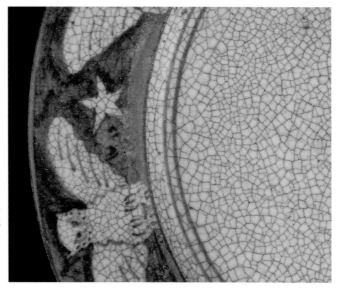

Rare grouse-pattern plate, stamp and impressed rabbit, 8 ¾", $2,500. (*Skinner*)

Horse chestnut-pattern plates, stamp and impressed rabbit, 8 ½", $300.

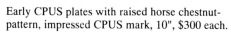

Early CPUS plates with raised horse chestnut-pattern, impressed CPUS mark, 10", $300 each.

Magnolia-pattern plates, stamp and impressed rabbit, 8 ½", $300, 6", $200.

Rare mushroom-pattern plate, stamp and impressed rabbit, 8 ½", $1,200.

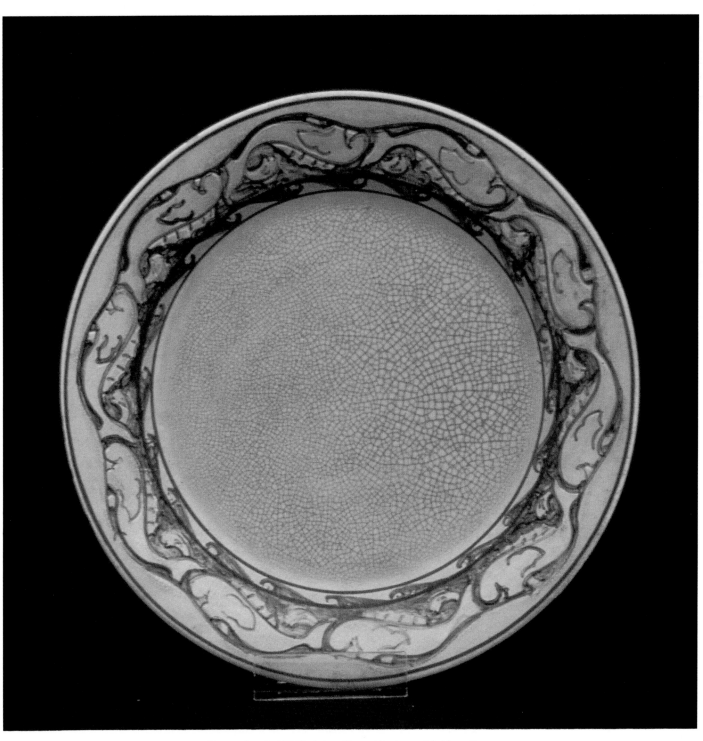

Rare and early CPUS plate with upside-down dolphin pattern,
initialed FC, impressed CPUS mark, 8 ¼", $1,200. (*Skinner*)

Grape-pattern plates, blue stamp and impressed rabbits, 8 ½", $200 each.

Azalea-pattern plates, blue stamp and double impressed rabbits, 8 ½", $300 each.

Iris-pattern items: 10" plate, $300; 8" plate, $200; 6" plate, $150; 4 ½" bowl, $150; cup and saucer, $300.

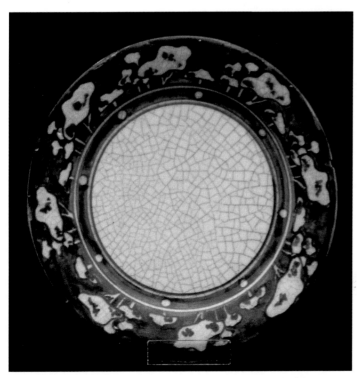

Snow tree-pattern plate, stamp and impressed rabbit, 8 ½", $300.

Unusual rabbit-pattern plate with monogram, stamp, and double-impressed rabbit, 8 ½", $500.

Rare poppy pattern plate, impressed rabbit, 8 ½", $1,000. (*Skinner*)

Unusual rabbit-pattern plates with tinted green and pink glazes, 8 ½", $400 each.

Rare lobster-pattern plate, stamp and double impressed rabbit, 6 ½", $400.

Rare pineapple-pattern plate, stamp and impressed rabbit, 8 ½", $600.

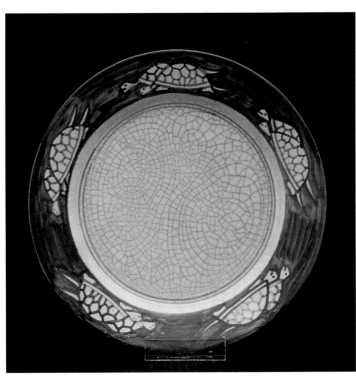

Turtle-pattern plate, stamp and double impressed rabbit, 8 ½", $600. (*Skinner*)

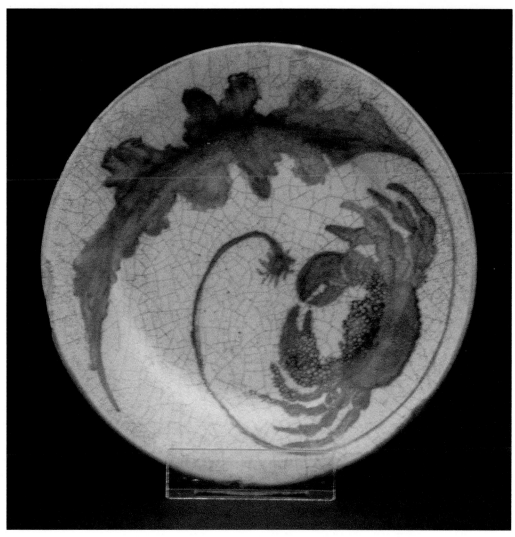

Rare Crab-pattern plate, stamp and impressed rabbit, 6 ½", $400.

Turkey pattern plates, stamp and impressed rabbit, 10", $400 each.

Unusual Dedham Pottery items: experimental daisy pattern plate, 6", $800; clover-pattern plate, 8 ½", $600; rare crackle-ware vase with butterfly and flowers, incised Dedham Pottery and HCR, 9" tall, $5,000; dolphin-pattern plate, 8 ½", $800; birds in potted orange tree plate, 6", $300.

Birds-in-potted-orange-tree-pattern stamp and impressed rabbit, 6 ½", $300. (*JMW Gallery*)

Swan-pattern plate, stamp and impressed rabbit, 8 ½", $300. (*JMW Gallery*)

Rare mushroom-pattern plate, stamp and
impressed rabbit, 8 ½", $900. (*JMW Gallery*)

Grape-pattern items: sugar and creamer, $475; demitasse cups and saucers, $150 each.

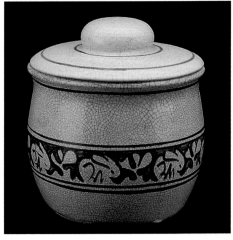

Rabbit-pattern covered sugar, $275.

Horse chestnut chocolate pot, $600; rabbit-pattern cup and saucer $150.

Rare rabbit-pattern covered tureens, incised Dedham Pottery, 9", $600 each. (*Skinner*)

Night-and-day pitcher, stamp, 5" tall, $600. (*JMW Gallery*)

Night side of the night-and-day pitcher.

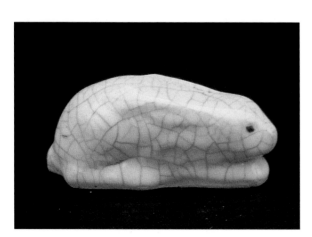

Dedham Pottery rabbit-form paperweight,
unsigned, 2 ¾" long, $475.

Grape-pattern cup, registered stamp, 3 ¼" tall,
$100; Grape-pattern tray, 9 ¾" x 6 ¼", $275.

Rabbit-pattern bowls, registered stamp, $100-150.

Rabbit-pattern covered sugar, $175;
Azalea-pattern sugar and creamer, $300.

Rabbit-pattern
mug, 7" tall,
$350.

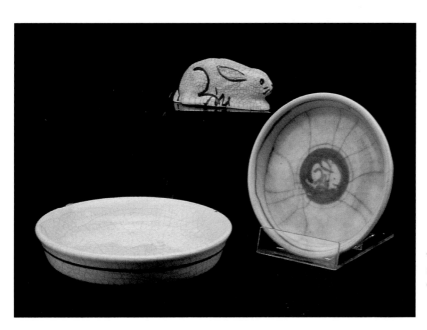

Three unusual Dedham Pottery items:
rabbit paperweight, $475; rabbit-pattern
dish, $200; undecorated dish, $100.

Unusual star-form dishes, $350 each.

Two rabbit-pattern trays, registered stamp, 10" long, $275 each.

Azalea-pattern creamer and covered sugar, 4 ¼" tall, $400. (*Skinner*)

Rare rabbit-pattern bowl with rabbit facing forward, 1 ¾" x 4 ¼", $250.

Unusual leaf-form bowl, 2 ½" tall x 5 ¼" diameter, $250.

Rare chick-pattern bowl, 2" x 4 ½", $400.

Swan-pattern pitcher, 5" tall, $300; candlesticks, 1 ½" tall, $300.

Lloyd E. Hawes, MD., *The Dedham Pottery and the Earlier Robertson's Chelsea Potteries*, from the 1968 exposition. A collectible itself, worth $100.

Chapter 3

J. & J.G. LOW ART TILE WORKS
(1878-1907)

Low Art Tile depicting cherubs, $125. (*JMW Gallery*)

The first mark used on Low Art Tiles.

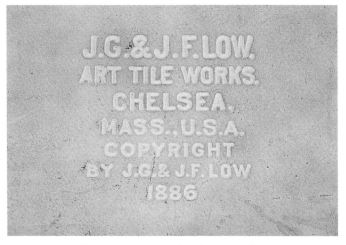

The second mark used on Low Art Tiles.

The Robertson family not only found the secrets of the lost Chinese glazes but also trained an employee so well he became their competition. John Gardner Low had studied landscape painting in Paris from 1858 to 1861. After attempting to earn a living as a painter in the United States, he began working for the Robertsons. There he learned the process of making pressed clay tiles and decorating them by pressing natural flowers into the moist clay and glazing over the imprints and relief. With the aid of his father, John Low, he opened his business, J. & J.G. Low Art Tile Works, in 1878. John G. managed to hire George Robertson away from Chelsea Keramic Art Works, who provided more expertise to the new firm. The tile works was located at 948 Broadway in Chelsea, Massachusetts, and fired for the first time in 1879.

It took the new company just over a year to win its first gold medal in 1880 at the Royal Manchester, Liverpool and North Lancashire Agricultural Society's exhibition in England. Many British tile manufacturers were also represented and their defeat by the fledgling American firm caused quite an upset. In January 1892, *Popular Science Monthly* stated:

"This record, probably unsurpassed in ceramic history, serves to illustrate the remarkably rapid development of an industry new in America, but old in the East; it shows the resources at command of the American potter."

Low's tiles with their pleasing glazes and impressed or relief designs were more favorable to Americans than painted tiles that were being imported from England. Low's tiles were incorporated into many commercial uses such as decorations for stoves, clock cases, fireplaces, and even soda fountains. Tiles ranged in size from two inches in diameter to six inches square. The decorations were mainly in the Japanese or Grecian manner with flowers, animals, statuary, historical figures, and geometric flourishes under a range of glossy glazes including yellow, green, blue, and brown. Although the tiles were "manufactured," Low's adherence to the ideal of the Arts and Crafts Movement was clear in his statement: "The beauty of it is that we never make two originals exactly alike in composition, although we can glaze them with identical colors or reproduce them by mechanical means." In 1883, John Low, John

Tiles depicting geometric, foliate designs, 6" square, $75 each. (*JMW Gallery*)

G. Low's father, retired from the business, and his grandson, John Farnsworth Low, joined the company. The pottery mark changed to J.G. & J.F. Low Art Tile Works. By the turn of the century, the taste for these glossy, relief-molded tiles changed in favor of new matte glazes. The Low Art Tile Works ceased production around 1902. J.G. Low died in 1907 and the firm's inventory was liquidated.

The most important contribution Low Art Tile Works made to the field of art pottery was its "plastic sketches." Arthur Osborne was an English sculptor who worked as a decorator for Low from 1879 until his return to England in 1893. These works were not commercial tiles like those incorporated into fireplaces but rather tiles that were to be considered fine art in themselves. An article in *The Century Magazine* on April 1882 described the process of their creation:

"The designs are first made in clay or wax, and a plaster cast is taken, which serves as a mold for the reproduction of any number desired. This mold is so formed that the design is depressed below the general surface of the cast just the required thickness of the tile. The sides are cut off even with the border of the design, leaving the ends by which to gauge the thickness of the tile, thus giving facilities for working the clay into the pattern and for lifting the tile from the plaster. The stock is mixed in the same way as for dust-tiles, only it is taken from the drying pan while it is yet moist enough to be plastic.

A quantity of this stock is taken by the molder, and beaten and kneaded on a block of plaster, which is kept damp enough to prevent it from drawing the moisture out of the clay. When it is of the proper consistency, the workman beats it out into a thin mass, smoothes the surface, lifts it with both hands, and flaps it over upon the mold, much as a cook puts pie crust upon a plate. He then works it with his thumb into the depressions of the plaster matrix and completes the operation by pressing clay into every part of the design by vigorous use of a wet sponge. The dry plaster soon absorbs the superfluous moisture from the clay and the tile becomes sufficiently rigid to be lifted from the mold. It may now be readily worked over by cutting tools. The pattern may be under-cut or perforated, or, indeed, elaborated to any desired degree. The drying and firing then follow, and the tile may be glazed with one color or with a combination of tints, according to the taste of the designer."

This process allowed for tiles to be up to twenty-four inches in height. Arthur Osborne signed tiles with his initials A.O., usually on the front of the tile. The photos at the end of the chapter, beginning on p.60, were taken from a period catalogue showing the plastic sketches available from the Low Art Tile Works. These tiles are very rare and sought after, ranging in value from $1,000-5,000.

Notice the range of colors in glazes available.

Low Art Tiles with floral designs in relief, 6" square, $125 each. (*JMW Gallery*)

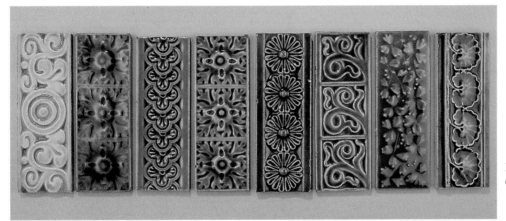

Border tiles with foliate designs, $50 each.

Low Art Tiles, 6" square, $75 each.

Low Art Tile, $50.

Border tiles with foliate designs, $50 each.

Low Art Tiles for stoves, $75 each.

Low Art tile $75.

Low Art Tiles, geometric floor tiles, $50 each.

Low Art Tile for fireplace surround, $150.

Low Art Tile depicting President Roosevelt, $225.

Low Art Tile with foliate designs from fireplace surround, $300 each.

Low Art Tile
exhibiting Japanese
influence, $150.
(*JMW Gallery*)

Unusual Low Art Tile receipt holder, $150. (*JMW Gallery*)

Low Art Tile depicting Ophelia, $375. (*JMW Gallery*)

Rare Low Art Tile in original iron frame, $2,000. (*JMW Gallery*)

Detail of frame's back.

Low Art Tiles with foliate designs, $225 pair.

Unusual Low Art Tile, $375. (*JMW Gallery*)

Low Art Tile, $375.

Low Art Tile, $200.

Low Art Tile, $150.

53

Low Art Tile, $175.

Unusual Low Art Tile in iron shelf, $375.

Low Art Tile, $250.

Low Art Tile depicting woman's face, $250; tile with cherubs, $375.

Low Art Tiles depicting cherubs, $400. (*Skinner*)

Rare Arthur Osborne Tile, notice AO cipher in lower right hand corner, $400.

Arthur Osborne Tile, $350. (*JMW Gallery*)

Low Art Tiles in Victorian velvet frames, $400 each.

Arthur Osborne Tile,
$475. (*JMW Gallery*)

Arthur Osborne plastic sketch, $1,800.

Plastic sketch entitled *Three of a Kind*, $1,500.

Plastic sketch entitled *After You, Sir*, $2,000.

Plastic sketch entitled *Fading Flowers*, $2,500.

59

direct from the artist's hands, without the glamour wrought by the glazing.

These sketches suggest the more extensive adaptation of this method to the production of picture-prints in process work. It certainly achieves an artistic effect which could hardly be arrived at in any other way: the firm, bold modelling with the contrasts of high lights and deep, rich shadows, and subtle *nuances* of rare delicacy. These could scarcely be obtained so successfully, in combination with an impression of firmness and substance, as by a photographic reproduction of a play of light over a modelled surface. We thus, by the aid of photography, enable one of the most attractive of artistic methods to be utilized in pictorial reproduction. The chief complaint against photography has been on account of its literalness. In reproductions of drawings, to some degree, it inevitably enfeebles the character of the original through loss of light and sharpness. But in photographically reproducing plastic work we obtain a permanent pictorial impression of effects which could otherwise only be enjoyed in the presence of the original. Then again, by lighting the subject from a different direction, it is possible to get quite another result from the same original.

One of these sketches, the dreamily poetical head called "When Age steals on," which was copied by process in a number of the Century magazine, several years ago, gave the first suggestion for the use of relief-modelling in clay as a method for magazine or book illustration. Since then this method has several times been used with excellent effect. The novelty of the idea made the results particularly taking, but the success was so genuine that it deserves to find permanent place among accepted methods. In the hands of a real artist, admirable illustrations might be achieved in this way, and the work would not be attended by any great technical difficulties.

Introduction to J. & J. G. Low's Plastic Sketch Book.

In estimating these works, their character, which is simply that of plastic *sketches*, should be borne in mind. Otherwise, some critical minds might perhaps be inclined to impeach the writer's soundness of art judgment for not calling attention to certain obvious defects in drawing or modelling,—the two terms may with propriety be used in reference to a method which makes use of both the picturesque and the plastic,—as if it were always the duty, or the province, of the critic to indicate the shortcomings of his subject, like one who, while calling attention to the beauty of a scene, should insist upon emphasizing some inharmonious feature which the superior charm of the whole naturally would make very subordinate and insignificant! But here the matter of defect does not enter into the question, for it would be an absurdity to look in a sketch for the finish of form which we would have the right to expect in a work claiming attention as a finished production. In the most famous sketches, by the greatest artists, crude and ill-defined forms are seldom lacking, and without them we should miss those elements of fresh, breezy vigor which give a sketch its value as an expression of a thought as it is first born into the mind, with the youthful dew and bloom fresh upon it.

These sketches show the action, the movement, which lends character to artistic effort, and which distinguishes the born artist from the laborious, unimaginative handworker who has learned his studio lessons, and to whom a prosaic correctness is the highest ideal. All that this sculptor does, is animate with this vivifying quality. It is particularly manifest in his delightful renderings of animals. We detect the evidences of a nice observation that has caught hundreds of little characteristic traits which give life to his subjects. It is qualities like these which bring to the true artist the admiration of the naturally sympathetic portion of the wider public as well as the

Introduction to J. & J. G. Low's Plastic Sketch Book.

appreciation of connoisseurs. Mark, for instance, in the sketch called "Recognition," such truthful details of movement as the lifted forefoot and raised head of the advancing horse, and the well-braced attitude of the other, his head and neck thrown back and cocked slightly aside, with the peculiar switch of the deficient tail. How admirably this is done, and with what simple beauty the quiet, pastoral landscape in all these works is rendered! Another characteristic quality is faithfully caught in "The Milky Way," where with gentle gait the cows are plodding homeward. And how thoroughly "A Windy Day" justifies its title! There is a whole gamut of nature's moods in these animal subjects.

The gentle humor of the artist is a trait that could not be overlooked. It has a kinship with that of the Japanese, as shown in those instances of the latter into which the element of caricature does not enter. "The Singing School," a subject quite in the Japanese manner, is an instance of this, as are the delightful "Donkey" subjects. How felicitously these latter are treated! How could the association of the idea of stupidity with the donkey, one of the most interesting and intelligent of animals, ever have originated?

A subject that can hardly fail to produce a merry laugh is the very expressive "Twelve o'Clock." Was the nature of the porker ever better depicted? Greediness pervades every feature; the huddling scramble, the hungrily agitated hindquarters, the eager twist of the tails, the forward lunge into the trough of the one on the right, and even the action of the one whose back is just seen beyond is complete.

The same quiet humor speaks in the *genre* subjects, which have much that suggests the old Dutch masters, without their coarseness, while they possess the domesticity of the English in this field without their sugary goodiness.

Introduction to J. & J. G. Low's Plastic Sketch Book.

Mr. Osborne is capital in giving character and expression to his figures, and he manages to convey a deal of meaning in his treatment of the hands, that crucial test of the true artist. Note, for instance, the action of the hands of the kindly faced old dame threading her needle in "Twilight," and of those of the characters in "Peace, My Children." The artist is also strikingly happy in his depiction of child-life, as in the swarms of naked and chubby little fellows in the admirably composed "Capturing the Snails," or the vivacious "When the Wind Blows."

The collection includes some strong character heads, like "Father Ignatius" and "An Egyptian Character," while a work like "Alceste" shows the artist's feeling for beauty of a classical simplicity. The many-sidedness of this sculptor's talent is surprising. His eclecticism is of the ideal kind; it is not imitative, but assimilative; his nature has given him a wide and retentive memory, and the impressions which he receives he digests thoroughly and reproduces in new and attractive forms. To survey the manifestations of an artist's mind, so fertile and so filled with quiet sunshine, is a rare and genuine pleasure.

SYLVESTER BAXTER.

Introduction to J. & J. G. Low's Plastic Sketch Book.

PLASTIC SKETCHES.

Introduction to J. & J. G. Low's Plastic Sketch Book.

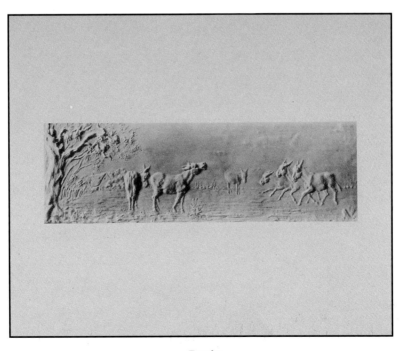

Eureka

Twelve o'Clock

Monk's Chanting

When Age Steals On

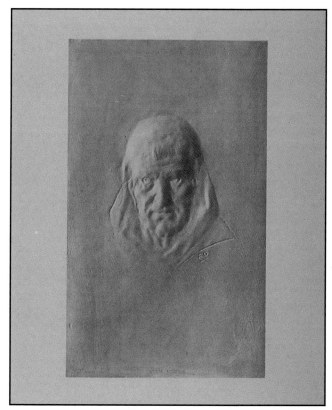

Father Ignatius

An Elizabethan Lady

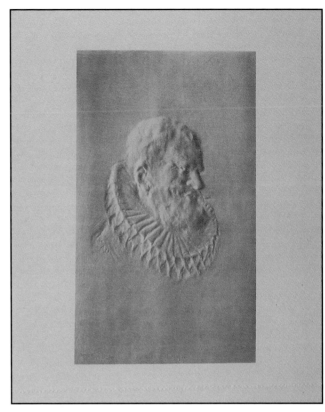

A Courtier of Elizabeth

1600

Ave Maria

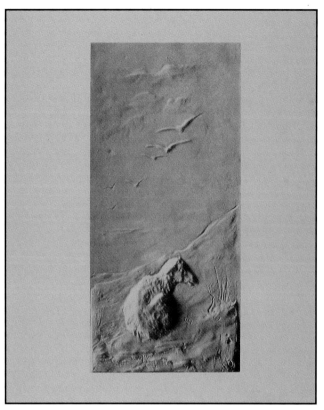

Solitude

Call to Breakfast

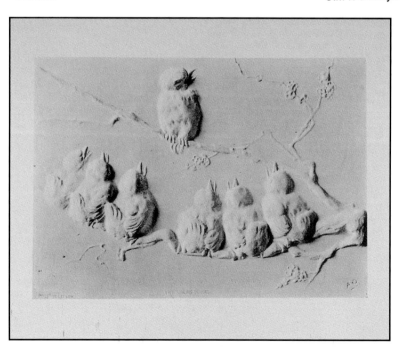

Singing School

Three of a Kind

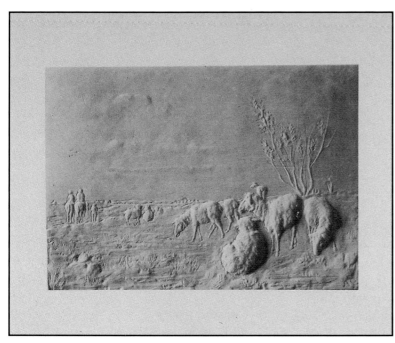

Morning

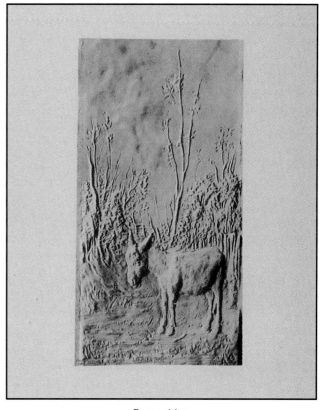

Recognition

A Windy Day

A Street in Normandy

From the Orient

66

Peace, My Children

When the Wind Blows

Discussing the Matter

An Egyptian Character (The Sheik)

Fading Flowers

To Apollo

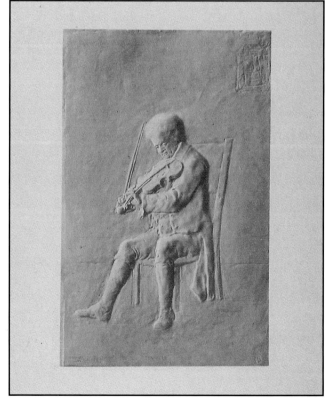

Tuning Up

68

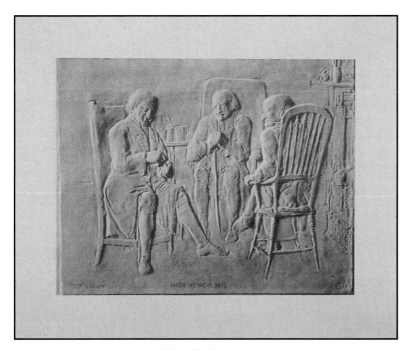

When We Were Boys

The Pathfinder

Twighlight

All the World

Rejected

No Thoroughfare

English Gypsies

The Milky Way

Going to Market

The Wind-Mill

71

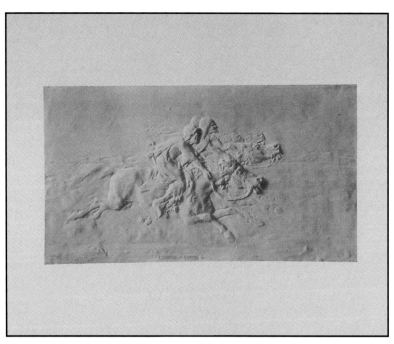

Escaping Simon

After You, Sir

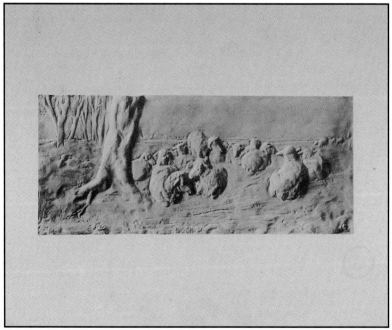

Noon

72

Chapter 4

GRUEBY POTTERY COMPANY

(1890-1920)

Exceptional decorated Grueby Pottery vase with yellow, glazed blossom.
Notice how the matte-green glaze on the body thins out on the leaves and
edges to create a more dynamic surface. $20,000. (*JMW Gallery*)

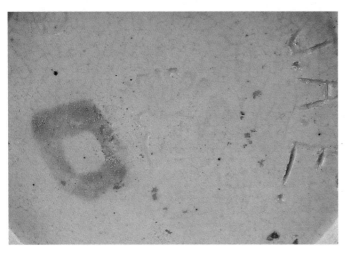

Grueby Pottery mark as found on the bottom of a vase.

Grueby Pottery mark as found on the bottom of a tile.

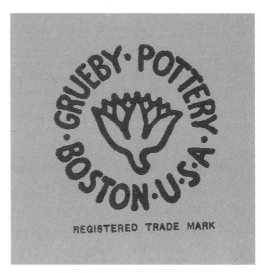

Grueby Pottery mark appearing on advertising pamphlet.

William H. Grueby worked in John G. Low's Art Tile Works for ten years. He learned press-tile technique sculpting from Arthur Osborne and glaze formulas from George Robertson. Possibly inspired by the success of his own employer, William left the Low Tile Works to establish his own firm in Revere, Massachusetts, in 1890. A fellow employee from the tile works, Eugene Atwood, joined William's fledgling firm under the name of Atwood & Grueby Co. They quickly associated themselves with the already established company of Fiske, Homes, and Company of Boston. This company acted as the agent and manager of the Boston Fire Brick Works. William was able to lease space from them for his company. He produced architectural installations similar to those of his former employer. Fiske, Homes and Company promoted the colored tiles of Atwood & Grueby Co.

William attended the World's Columbian Exposition, Chicago, in 1893 as Fiske's representative. There William would be exposed to some of the world's leading ceramists. He was influenced by the representation of Persian design and the avant-garde French potters Ernest Chaplet and Auguste Delaherche, who concentrated on simple forms and monochromatic glazes. William became dissatisfied with his business and looked to create a better venue for his ambitions.

The Atwood & Grueby Company was dissolved in 1894. The Grueby Faience Company is first listed in the Boston directory of 1894. In 1895, William would return to the Midwest to tour the major pottery manufacturers. *The Clayworker* magazine stated the following in 1895:

> "William H. Grueby, President of the Grueby Faience Co., Boston, looked in on The Clayworker recently. He has made quite an extensive trip through the Central States for the purpose of examining machinery, kilns, etc. His company will soon add the manufacture of hollow and porous fire-proofing to their other lines, and they want the best and most modern equipment they can secure. They now make a large variety of glazed and enameled architectural terra-cotta of rare artistic character."

The Midwestern pottery companies must have inspired William to pursue a line of pottery vessels.

The Grueby Faience Company was incorporated on June 2, 1897. William was the general manager of the pottery and he enlisted two important business partners: William Hagerman Graves and George Prentiss Kendrick. Graves was a wealthy young graduate of Massachusetts Institute of Technology in 1892. Kendrick was a craftsmen involved with the Boston Society of Arts and Crafts and a designer for a prestigious firm. While Graves served as Grueby's business manager, Kendrick would provide the important role of designing Grueby's new art pottery line.

In the first exhibition of the Boston Society of Arts and Crafts in 1897, Grueby Faience Company exhibited several items. The two most notable were Moorish tiles with a matte glaze and a cylindrical vase with a floral motif. The matte glazes on the tiles were a complete change from the glossy tiles that were produced at the Low Art Tile Works. Grueby most likely utilized his experience of Chaplet and Delaherche's works at the Columbian Exposition in Chicago in these works. The combination of this matte glaze with the forms designed by Kendrick for pottery would make Grueby Faience Company an international success.

Kendrick's designs employed the Arts and Crafts ideals. The exhibition catalogue from the 1899 Boston Society of Arts and Crafts show best describe these ideals as:

"1. Every form must be perfectly adapted to the use for which it is intended.... Eccentricity of form is to be avoided as vulgar.

2. Every form should be in harmony with the material in which it is executed. It should indeed be the outcome of a thorough knowledge and sensitive appreciation of the habits of the material used, and of the methods of the particular craft employed.

3. The decoration put upon any object must be in harmony with its form. The more intimate relation between the form of the object and its decoration, the more beautiful it will be."

Kendrick seemed to have no problem conforming to these guidelines. This was confirmed in the Paris exposition of 1900 in which Grueby Faience Company won two gold medals.

Kendrick left the firm in 1903 and Addison Le Boutillier was hired full-time to carry out designs for tiles and specialty projects, and to be in charge of all the modellers. The modeling of the pottery was carried out by young female graduates of Boston's Museum of Fine Arts School, the Massachusetts Normal School, and the Cowles Art School. An article in the Boston Globe newspaper described the process:

"When the smooth, damp vase comes to the hands of the young woman decorator the outline of leaf or flower to be employed in decorating is drawn lightly in freehand with a small apple wood implement. Then a piece of clay is rolled out to a rope about the size of a knitting needle, and the outline of a leaf, for example, is laid on the vase. It is then pressed out on the inner side and rounded up on the outer, until the perfect leaf is formed. When flowers are made the same method is followed except in the detail of modeling."

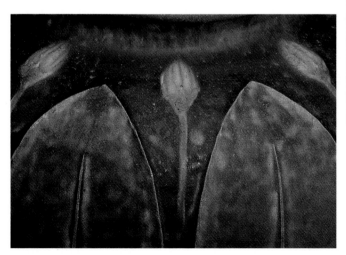

Although the decorators followed designs, each piece produced was distinctive of that person's efforts. An advertising pamphlet produced by the Grueby Company stressed this point: "Instead of the mechanical formality, which has so often been mistaken for precision, every surface and line of this ware evinces the appreciative touch of the artist's hand." After the modeling was complete, the vessel would be glazed with one of the matte enamels. It seems that Grueby's discovery of these crackle glazes probably stemmed from knowledge he gained while working for Low, where George Robertson brought his vast knowledge of glaze formulations to the company. In any case, Grueby expanded on these glazes, producing them in a variety of colors such as green, blue, yellow, and brown and utilized them in combinations of yellow buds on green backgrounds.

Grueby Pottery vase exhibiting a powerful form that accentuates the vertical emphasis, notice the places where the glaze skips, creating light spots, even with these glaze skips that sometimes can affect value, this vessel approaches the $30,000-plus category. (*JMW Gallery*)

Left:
Detail of Grueby Pottery vase showing the vibrant yellow glazed buds and the well-defined edges of the leaves and buds.

The importance of his glazes was apparent in the price paid for two vases in 1903 by the Worcester Art Museum, Massachusetts. The two vases were exactly the same form and height, but one exhibited a matte-white color while the other displayed a crackling, matte-green glaze. The matte-white vase was $12 while the dynamic matte-green one was $75. William Graves describes the decoration:

"The Grueby Pottery differs from historical precedents not so much in the method of making as in decoration and texture. The undecorated pieces depend for effect upon whatever character may be given them on the potter's wheel, combined with any special beauty there may be in the color and texture, just as in the case of the Oriental examples. In other pieces we have aimed at further decorative effect by modeling on them appropriate ornament in low relief, the crispness of which is softened and given a fictile character by the thick opaque enamels. Our direct precedent and inspiration for this style of decoration was the work of the famous French potter Delahersche, whose kilns are at Beauvais."

The popularity of the matte glazes brought out many imitators. Grueby's designs became fairly repetitive after Kendrick left the firm in 1903. Most major art pottery companies began to produce a line of matte-glazed, molded pottery which was made quickly and cheaply. William H. Grueby's company would begin to fall apart. The art pottery component of the company was incorporated under Grueby Pottery Company. The tile manufacturing became Grueby Faience. By 1909, both would be in financial disaster and the final sale of Grueby items occurred in November, 1910, at the Boston Craftsman showroom at 470 Boylston Street. William attempted to resurrect the tile manufacturing, but finally sold it to C. Pardee Works of Perth Amboy, New Jersey. William continued to manage the faience line for Pardee until his death in February 1925.

The works of William H. Grueby have become favorites among arts and crafts collectors today. The harmonious combination of color that occurs from mixing matte glazes with fumed oak inspired the famous furniture maker Gustav Stickley to incorporate Grueby tiles into his furniture. This harmonious look has also inspired collectors to pay a premium price for exceptionally glazed items. Recently a small 4 ½-inch vase sold for more than $20,000 at auction. The prices for this pottery have more than tripled during the last ten years.

A smaller Grueby vase with the same decoration. The matte-green glaze on the body exhibits more of an alligator-skin effect than the smoother glaze on the taller version. $15,000. (*JMW Gallery*)

Detail of Grueby vase decoration. The buds on this vase have an almost radioactive yellow effect rather than the more typical, subdued yellow glaze treatments on buds and flowers.

Grueby Pottery vase with bud and leaf treatment. The buds lack the vibrancy of other vessels, yet the subtle effect of the thinning edges on the leaves presents a pleasing presence. $8,000. (*JMW Gallery*)

Grueby Pottery vase with butterscotch glaze, $6,000. (*Skinner*)

Grueby Pottery vase emphasizing a vertical thrust with thick matte-green glaze and good definition on buds, $12,000. (*Skinner*)

Left:
Grueby Pottery vase exhibiting a broader leaf that is somewhat awkward, but the thinning glaze and bold yellow glaze on the bud bring the composition together, $7,000. (*Skinner*)

Opposit page:
Rare Grueby Pottery vase with blue matte glaze, $30,000. (*Skinner*)

Grueby Pottery vase with unusual decoration, $3,000. (*Skinner*)

Grueby Pottery vase showing how the yellow glaze can run off the flower when being fired, although a rare item, this does affect its value, $3,000. (*Skinner*)

Before Tiffany Studios began to produce its own pottery items they would order lamp bases to mount their shades on. This lamp exhibits the harmony between a Tiffany acorn-pattern shade and a Grueby leaf-pattern base, $20,000. (*Skinner*)

Grueby Pottery lamp with
Tiffany Studios shade,
$20,000. (*Skinner*)

Be careful when examining Grueby Lamp bases.
Sometimes the lamp fixtures were placed inside
the vessels with spring loaded mechanisms. If you
try remove them, you will break the vase. $8,000.
(*Skinner*)

Grueby Pottery lamp base
with Tiffany Studios shade,
$12,000. (*Skinner*)

Exceptional Grueby Pottery vase with one of the most dramatic organic forms in American pottery, complemented by a smooth butterscotch glaze, $30,000-plus. (*Skinner*)

Grueby Pottery vase showing the same form with dark matte-green glaze, $30,000-plus. (*Skinner*)

Grueby Pottery vase with dramatic vertical form, smooth even, matte-green glaze, $20,000-plus. (*JMW Gallery*)

Grueby Pottery vase again showing a vertical emphasis in form that seems somewhat awkward, $8,000. (*Skinner*)

Grueby Pottery cylindrical vase, $4,000. (*JMW Gallery*)

Grueby Pottery vase with thick matte-green glaze, $2,500. (*Skinner*)

Grueby Pottery
vase, $7,000.
(*Skinner*)

84

Grueby Pottery vase,
$8,000. (*Skinner*)

Rare Grueby Pottery vase with vertical form, rich matte-green
glaze thinning precisely at edges, $25,000-plus. (*Skinner*)

Grueby Pottery vase
with nice bold form,
$7,500. (*Skinner*)

Grueby Pottery vase in which the curled form
accentuates the leaf decoration, $6,000. (*Skinner*)

Grueby Pottery cabinet vase, $300.

Grueby Potter
vase with incised
decoration
presenting a
modern form,
$3,000.

Grueby Pottery vase with broad leaves, $3,000. (*Skinner*)

Grueby Pottery vase with thick dripping alligator glaze, $2,500. (*Skinner*)

Grueby Pottery
vase with glaze
skips. $800.

Grueby Pottery vase with nicely thinning
glaze at edges, $4,000. (*JMW Gallery*)

Grueby Pottery vase with
deep matte-green glaze,
$8,000. (*JMW Gallery*)

Grueby Pottery vase,
$3,000. (*Skinner*)

Grueby Pottery vase, $2,000. (*Skinner*)

Grueby Pottery
vase with
vertical leaf
decoration,
$4,500.

Grueby Pottery vase with light-green matte glaze, $6,000. (*Skinner*)

Grueby Pottery vase with unusual form, probably for lamp base, $4,000. (*JMW Gallery*)

Grueby Pottery vase exhibiting dynamic
smoky brown glaze, $10,000. (*Skinner*)

Grueby Pottery vase with light-green
matte glaze, $2,500. (*Skinner*)

Grueby Pottery bowl with thick dripping matte green glaze, $2,000. (*Skinner*)

Grueby Pottery vase with broad leaf decoration, $4,000.

Grueby Pottery vase with butterscotch glaze on an Oriental form, $3,500.

Grueby Pottery vase with dark blue glaze, $4,000. (*Skinner*)

Grueby Pottery scarab paperweight, $450. (*JMW Gallery*)

Grueby Pottery
vase with
unusual blue
glaze, $3,000.

Grueby Pottery vase exhibiting an unusual white crackle glaze similar to those by Hugh Robertson at Chelsea Keramic Art Works, $5,000. (*Skinner*)

Unusual Grueby Pottery vase with high glaze, $500.

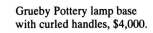
Grueby Pottery lamp base
with curled handles, $4,000.

Grueby Pottery covered vase with rare alligator blue glaze, $5,000. (*Skinner*)

Grueby Pottery tulip tile,
when the edges are glazed it
means they were never
meant to be set into a wall,
usually these were made as
trivets on tables, $1,200.
(*JMW Gallery*)

Grueby Pottery pond lily tile, $1,500. (*Skinner*)

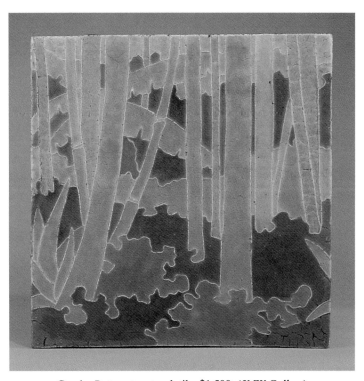

Grueby Pottery tree trunk tile, $1,500. (*JMW Gallery*)

Grueby Pottery pine tree tile, $1,500. (*JMW Gallery*)

Grueby Pottery tree tile, retailed as
Nursery tiles, $1,500. (*JMW Gallery*)

Grueby Pottery turtle tile with
butterscotch glaze, $1,500. (*Skinner*)

Grueby Pottery turtle tiles with green glaze, $1,500 each. (*Skinner*)

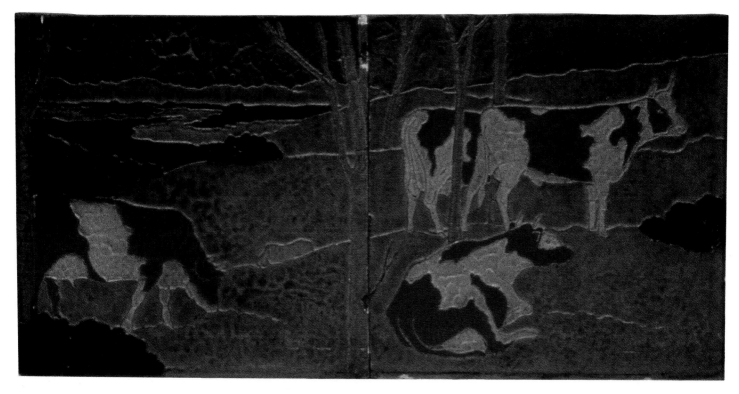

Rare Grueby Pottery tiles of cows grazing, $10,000-plus. (*Skinner*)

Grueby Pottery horses tile, these tiles would repeat as a border over plain matte glazed tiles suggested for use in a bathroom, $1,200. (*Skinner*)

Grueby Pottery knight tile, exhibits a range of color in matte glazes, $1,800. (*Skinner*)

Grueby Pottery mermaid tile, described as tile No. 657 in the Grueby catalogue which states these are modeled in low relief, in one or more colors, or with depressed-parts-only glazed; used singly, in groups, or to form borders. Sizes: 6", 4", 3" squares, and 3" and 2" hexagons, $450. (*Skinner*)

98

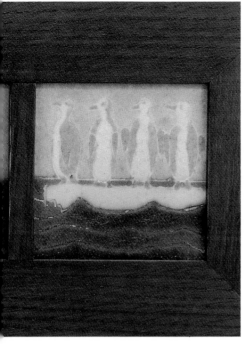

Grueby Pottery animal tiles, wonderful figures in ocean scenes, $1,200 each. (*JMW Gallery*)

Grueby Pottery Viking ship tile, $2,500. (*JMW Gallery*)

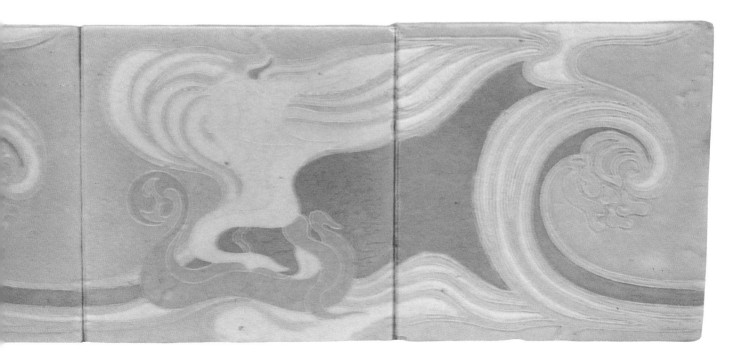

Grueby Pottery ship tile frieze, $5,000. (*Skinner*)

Grueby Pottery Palm Tree Frieze, $20,000-plus. (*Skinner*)

Grueby Pottery geometric-pattern border tiles, $350 each. (*JMW Gallery*)

Grueby Pottery floor tiles, collected today to frame together or to accent new tiles that are being installed, $25-75 each. (*JMW Gallery*)

Gustav Stickley table with inset Grueby tiles, $30,000. (*Skinner*)

Grueby advertising pamphlet

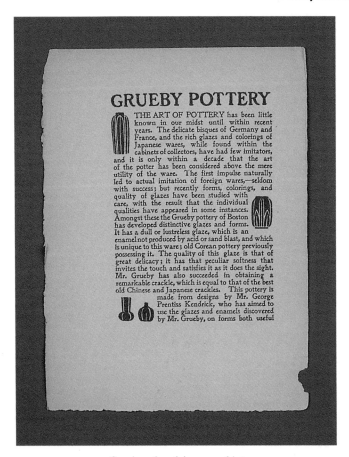

GRUEBY POTTERY

THE ART OF POTTERY has been little known in our midst until within recent years. The delicate bisques of Germany and France, and the rich glazes and colorings of Japanese wares, while found within the cabinets of collectors, have had few imitators, and it is only within a decade that the art of the potter has been considered above the mere utility of the ware. The first impulse naturally led to actual imitation of foreign wares,—seldom with success; but recently forms, colorings, and quality of glazes have been studied with care, with the result that the individual qualities have appeared in some instances. Amongst these the Grueby pottery of Boston has developed distinctive glazes and forms. It has a dull or lustreless glaze, which is an enamel not produced by acid or sand blast, and which is unique to this ware; old Corean pottery previously possessing it. The quality of this glaze is that of great delicacy; it has that peculiar softness that invites the touch and satisfies it as it does the sight. Mr. Grueby has also succeeded in obtaining a remarkable crackle, which is equal to that of the best old Chinese and Japanese crackles. This pottery is made from designs by Mr. George Prentiss Kendrick, who has aimed to use the glazes and enamels discovered by Mr. Grueby, on forms both useful

Grueby advertising pamphlet

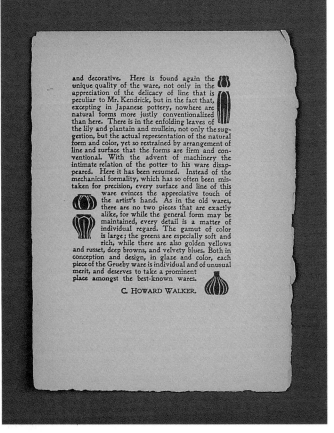

and decorative. Here is found again the unique quality of the ware, not only in the appreciation of the delicacy of line that is peculiar to Mr. Kendrick, but in the fact that, excepting in Japanese pottery, nowhere are natural forms more justly conventionalized than here. There is in the enfolding leaves of the lily and plantain and mullein, not only the suggestion, but the actual representation of the natural form and color, yet so restrained by arrangement of line and surface that the forms are firm and conventional. With the advent of machinery the intimate relation of the potter to his ware disappeared. Here it has been resumed. Instead of the mechanical formality, which has so often been mistaken for precision, every surface and line of this ware evinces the appreciative touch of the artist's hand. As in the old wares, there are no two pieces that are exactly alike, for while the general form may be maintained, every detail is a matter of individual regard. The gamut of color is large; the greens are especially soft and rich, while there are also golden yellows and russet, deep browns, and velvety blues. Both in conception and design, in glaze and color, each piece of the Grueby ware is individual and of unusual merit, and deserves to take a prominent place amongst the best-known wares.

C. HOWARD WALKER.

Grueby advertising pamphlet

Chapter 5

HAMPSHIRE POTTERY
(1897-1923)

Hampshire Pottery vase with matte-blue glaze
and leaf decoration, $1,200. (*JMW Gallery*)

Hampshire Pottery vase with smooth matte-green glaze, $800. (*JMW Gallery*)

Hampshire Pottery mark as found on the bottom of a vase.

In 1871, James Scullay Taft and his uncle, James Burnap, purchased the Milestone Mills, a former clothespin factory in Keene, New Hampshire, with money earned from a grocery business. They chose the site because of the fine raw materials available in the area for producing pottery. However, before Taft could begin producing his wares, the structure burnt to the ground. A new building was quickly erected and the production of utilitarian wares began a few months later.

Taft employed the talents of Mr. Tom Stanley, formerly of England, in 1879. He brought with him the knowledge of majolica-type glazes. He convinced Taft of the commercial potential of this ware and began producing decorative products along with stoneware jugs, molasses jugs,

and crocks. The decorative ware became so successful that Taft built a new kiln for the firing of the majolica glazes. The new kiln also allowed them to produce an underglaze slip decoration similar to Rookwood Pottery. A Vermont artist, Wallace King, was brought into the company to manage the production of this ware.

In 1904, Cadmon Robertson (the brother-in-law of James Taft) joined the company. Cadmon wasn't a relative of the famous Robertsons of Chelsea, Massachusetts, but certainly he must have been aware of their work. Educated as a chemist and a member of the Boston Society of Arts and Crafts, he created more than nine hundred glaze formulas for the Hampshire Pottery Company. The glazes were similar to

Hampshire Pottery vase
with leaf decoration,
$750. (*JMW Gallery*)

Hampshire Pottery vase with
green/brown striated glaze,
$700. (*JMW Gallery*)

both Low Art Tile Works and Grueby Pottery, which resulted in great commercial success. The forms of vessels were molded rather than hand thrown, cutting down on expenses. Some forms were almost identical to Grueby Pottery.

Wallace King retired in 1908 after twenty-five years of service to the company. Cadmon died in 1914 and the company lost its two most creative influences. James Taft decided to sell the company in 1916 to George M. Morton. Morton was also a member of the Boston Society of Arts and Crafts and a former employee of the Grueby Pottery Company. Morton expanded the range of glazes on Hampshire Pottery, undoubtedly borrowing from his experiences with the Robertson's glazes at Grueby. The company abruptly closed with the onset of World War I. After the war, Morton resumed operations, but limited the company to hotel china and tiles. The cost of coal became too ex-

pensive for the company to remain competitive and operations ceased in 1923.

Among today's collectors, Hampshire Pottery does not demand the same prices as those of Grueby Pottery. Although Cadmon Robertson was given the title of Master Craftsman by the Boston Society of Arts and Crafts in 1908, the firm produced molded items and seemed to be responding to commercial demand rather than an inherent love of craft. Whether Grueby Pottery was doing the same seems to be a matter of opinion. By 1911, Grueby's employees were punching time clocks and were distinguished as employees rather than modelers. The marketing machine of Grueby Pottery that secured gold medals during the period is probably more responsible for the disparity in prices today than the actual items themselves. In any case, Hampshire Pottery remains a good buy for collectors of art pottery today.

Hampshire Pottery vase, $450. (*JMW Gallery*)

Hampshire Pottery dark matte-green vase. Notice how thick the glaze is on the base, $600. (*JMW Gallery*)

Hampshire Pottery vase with feathered blue glaze, $1,200. (*JMW Gallery*)

Unusual Hampshire Pottery vase that shows some of the pottery's works are dynamic and innovative. This example displays three types of glazes for decoration, $1,800. (*Skinner*)

Hampshire Pottery vase, $450. (*JMW Gallery*)

107

Hampshire Pottery vase with deep-blue matte glaze, $600. (*JMW Gallery*)

Hampshire Pottery bowl with leaf-and-bud pattern, $750. (*JMW Gallery*)

108

Hampshire Pottery
vase with leaf and
flower design, $600.

Hampshire Pottery vase with incised design, $350. (*JMW Gallery*)

109

Hampshire Pottery vase with dynamic brown-and-black alligator glaze, $650. (*JMW Gallery*)

Hampshire Pottery vase with dynamic green-and-blue alligator glaze, $650. (*JMW Gallery*)

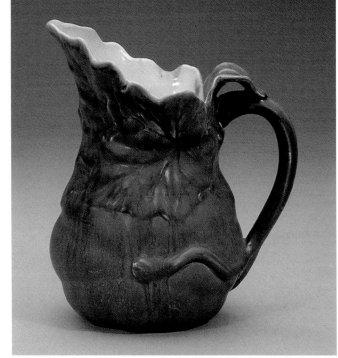

Hampshire Pottery pitcher with leaf-and-vine design, $475. (*Skinner*)

Hampshire
Pottery pitcher,
$200. (*JMW Gallery*)

Hampshire Pottery jar, $475. (*JMW Gallery*)

Hampshire Pottery candlestick, $475. (*JMW Gallery*)

111

Hampshire Pottery also provided bases for shades. Here a simple, leaded-glass shade provides a pleasing presence for a tenth of the price of a Grueby lamp, $2,000. (*Skinner*)

Detail of lamp base showing a conventionalized organic form.

Hampshire Pottery lamp, $2,500. (*Skinner*)

Chapter 6

THE WORK OF RUSSELL G. CROOK

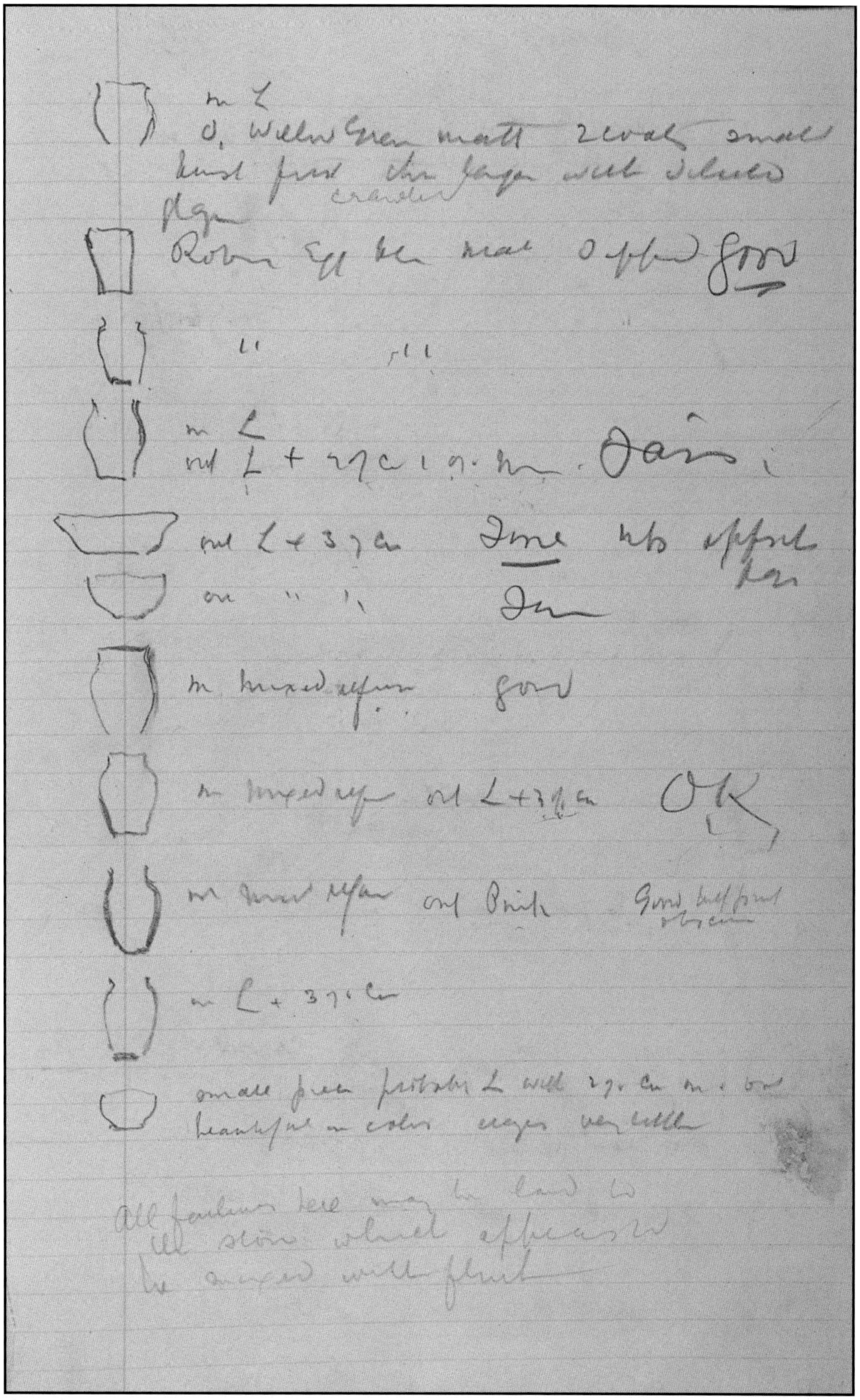

Sketches of
designs from
Russell Crook's
sketch book.

THE NEW YORK STATE SCHOOL OF CLAY-WORKING & CERAMICS
AT ALFRED UNIVERSITY
ALFRED, N.Y.
CHARLES F. BINNS, Director

September 8th. 1910

Mr. Russell G. Crook,

South Lincoln, Mass.

Dear Mr. Crook:-

I have your letter of 5th. inst. and will try to reply to your enquiries although I will confess at the outset that my experience with salt glazing is very small. At the same time there are certain phenomena which belong indifferently to every description of clay work.

I presume you have tried the under-glaze colors which are sold on the market and are not satisfied with them. I think you should get some very refractory clay such as Florida clay mis-called a kaolin. Mix this with your cobalt oxide and calcine the mixture in the hottest part of your kiln. Then grind fine and use as a pigment. In painting on the green clay it is best to mix a little of the unburned clay body with the color to make it adhere and to help in securing a uniform shrinkage. The proportion of cobalt in the mix will depend on the strength you need the color. I think from your reports that you have been using the blue too strong. The cobalt is apt to blacken when too thick.

The dark color of the body is probably due to a reducing fire. Salt glazing seems to demand this condition but I am not

at all sure that it is necessary. The old English salt glaze does not show signs of reduction and the brown ware of Cologne would have been dark gray if the fire had been reducing. It might be worth while to try the effect of a clear burn, getting all the air possible in the kiln and cooling slowly in as good a current of air as can be obtained.

As to your last question I presume you mean to ask if I think it possible to make a living at this work. I do not say that it is not possible but my opinion is that the higher a man's ideals are the more difficult it is. I know a man who sells almost everything he makes but then he makes what will sell. Mr. Baggs has done well in his line but it is a much less expensive one than yours. On the other hand you have the field to yourself and the attempt is well worth while.

I wish you could find the time to come here for even a week or two. I feel sure we could solve some of your difficulties much better than by writing. However do not be afraid to write as fully as you care to.

Yours very truly,

An important correspondence between Charles Binns, one of the most important potters of the time period, and Russell Crook, which emphasizes the uniqueness of his product and the struggle of an artist.

Information on the life of Russell G. Crook is scarce at best. It is known that he was a member of the Boston Society of Arts and Crafts, which listed him as a sculptor, plaster modeler, and potter. He was designated as a Craftsmen and exhibitor in 1899 and was given the title Master Craftsman in 1908. His address changed from Boston in 1900 to South Lincoln, Massachusetts, between 1902 and 1927.

It is also known that Crook designed tiles for William Grueby. A major commission by the Grueby Company was the decorating of Dreamworld (the lavish estate of Thomas Lawson in Scituate, Massachusetts) in 1902. An article in *The Brickbuilder* magazine describes Crook's design:

Russell Crook mark as found on the bottom of a vase.

"...conventionalized bunches of grapes, ears of corn, and other farm products. The [Tiffany] chandelier is a huge pumpkin, and the breakfast alcove chandelier and also the wall brackets are made up of pumpkin blossoms and leaves in their natural colors. To harmonize with this, the fireplace starts on each side with a huge, golden pumpkin on a very dark blue background. On this background the vine wanders over the top with its green leaves and bright yellow blossoms and even flows out on to the hearth with a few leaves that seem to keep the pumpkin just where it was intended to be. By means of these dull tones the fireplace, although singing in the highest tones of yellow and green, still remains a fire-

place facing on the same plane as the wall paneling and embracing two huge bears by Crook that form the andirons."

Crook was evidently a talented individual who understood the principles of creating an arts and crafts interior. But Crook's talents went beyond that of design and into the vessels he created himself.

Most American art pottery finds its influences in the international aesthetic movement during the turn of the century. This has been argued convincingly by Professor Martin Eidelberg who states that, "American ceramics reveal the same development and were produced with the same variety of styles as their European counterparts." A

114

good example of this is the comparison between the ceramics of William Grueby and the French potter August Delaherche which display the same forms and organic-style glazes. The glaze craze that developed in the New England area during the turn of the century is thought to be nothing more than the manifestation of a more structured organic Art Nouveau form. But the vessels of Russell Crook seem to contradict this view of American ceramics.

Crook's vessels are a salt-glazed stoneware reminiscent of stoneware produced in New York and New England during the mid to late 1800s. The decoration consists of repeated designs on simple forms. The designs are of fantastic animals which seem to be created by painting cobalt around a stencil. His work was certainly part of the Arts and Crafts movement but seems to show little debt to European stylistic developments.

The works of Russell Crook are extremely rare and have not surfaced frequently enough to properly place values on them. Hopefully with further research and discoveries, a greater appreciation of these works will be attained.

Russell Crook vase with unusual design of elephants. (*JMW Gallery*)

Back of vase.

Russell Crook vase with undulating fish. (*JMW Gallery*)

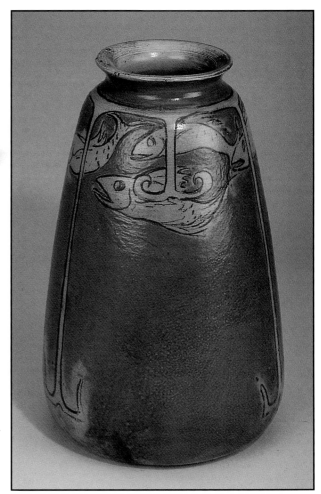

Back of vase.

Russell Crook vase with
horsemen and cattle.
(*JMW Gallery*)

Back of vase.

Russell Crook vase with moose. (*JMW Gallery*)

Back of vase.

Russell Crook vase with deer. (*JMW Gallery*)

Back of vase.

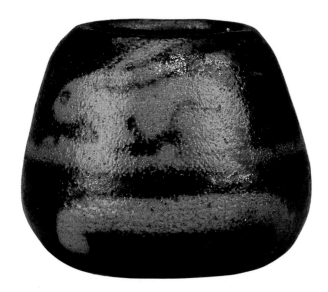

Russell Crook vase with rabbit. Notice how similar the pattern is to Dedham Pottery. (*JMW Gallery*)

Russell Crook vase with birds. (*JMW Gallery*)

119

Russell Crook vase forms. (*JMW Gallery*)

Russell Crook bowl with Greek design. (*JMW Gallery*)

Opposite page:
Russell Crook vase with Greek design,
probably inspired by items in the Museum
of Fine Arts, Boston. (*JMW Gallery*)

121

Russell Crook ship tile. (*JMW Gallery*)

Russell Crook tile, (*JMW Gallery*)

Russell Crook tile. (*JMW Gallery*)

Chapter 7

MERRIMAC POTTERY COMPANY
(1902-1908)

Merrimac Pottery vase with overlapping leaf design,
deep matte-green glaze, $1,200. (*JMW Gallery*)

Merrimac Pottery vase
with ruffled edge, $300.

Merrimac
Pottery mark
as found on
the bottom of
a vase.

The Merrimac Ceramic Company began its existence in 1897, producing flower pots and other utilitarian wares in Newburyport, Massachusetts. Its founder, Thomas S. Nickerson, studied in England and was probably familiar with the teachings of John Ruskin. He was recognized by the Boston Society of Arts and Crafts as a craftsman in 1899 and a Master Craftsman in 1902.

Also that year, the name of the company was changed to Merrimac Pottery Company. Glazes became more complex and a variety of colors and glazes appeared. The vessels displayed simple classic forms and organic foliate designs. The pottery also produced classical garden pottery and redware based on pottery of the Roman Empire. The company received a silver medal at the St. Louis exposition in 1904.

Merrimac is an art pottery company that suffered from the success of its nearby competitor, Grueby. It was accused of copying the Boston company's glazes. The Newburyport *Daily News* stated in 1903 in defense of the pottery:

"That accusation is not borne out by a careful study and comparison of both wares. Save in the color of certain green pieces, the resemblance is very little; and really the greens of Merrimac, so far as one writer has observed, are not at all comparable

to Grueby, with its soft, kid-glove-like surface and finish. The Merrimac has, however, so much to offer in scope of variety (and this cannot be said of Grueby) that very interesting and charming products come up for consideration quite independent of the green specimens. Many of the Merrimac pieces show a cheerful, tender, bright, radiant character, which is wholly lacking in the Grueby. The soft color of the Merrimac is especially pleasing and the metallic glow on some of the articles is most effective, rich and brilliant. This metallic finish is the finer and more acceptable, as seen upon the low-tone pieces, such as on the soft, dull violet, rose, and similar colorings."

Merrimac was well accomplished and produced organic glazes that in some respects are superior to Grueby Pottery. The success of Merrimac Pottery would probably be more recognized if a fire had not destroyed the works in October of 1908.

Items of Merrimac Pottery can be found with a paper label or an impressed mark of a sturgeon. Merrimac is an Indian word meaning sturgeon. The Merrimac green glaze is distinctive, having a vibrancy that one does not see on Grueby or Hampshire. The company's short existence makes the pottery hard to find.

Merrimac Pottery vase with rust-color glaze, $3,000. (*JMW Gallery*)

Merrimac Pottery mug, $300. (*JMW Gallery*)

Merrimac Pottery vase with matte-yellow glaze, $600. (*JMW Gallery*)

Merrimac Pottery
vase with feathered
green glaze, this
glaze can be found
on unmarked items
that can be attributed
to Merrimac, $1,000.
(*Skinner*)

Chapter 8

WALLEY POTTERY

(1898-1919)

Walley Pottery vase
with thick, sliding
glaze that has the
effect of alligator
skin, $10,000.
(*Collection of Rod
Mckenzie*)

ART POTTERY

Detail of Walley Pottery vase with quatrefoil
opening creating a dramatic, organic effect.

Walley Pottery sign that stood in front of
the shop in West Sterling, Massachusetts.

Walley Pottery mark as found
on the bottom of a vase.

William J. Walley was born in Ohio in 1852. When
his father died, the family moved to England where, at the
age of ten, Walley began working at the Minton Ceramics
Factory. After eleven years of grueling work, from 1862-
1873, he was well trained in all aspects of working a pottery company.

At twenty-one years of age, Walley returned to the
United States and worked for a pottery in Maine. After a
short stay he moved down to Worcester, Massachusetts,
to work at the old F.B. Norton Pottery Company which
began in 1858. The Norton Company was famous for its
stoneware salt-glazed jugs. They also produced some
stoneware items in natural forms such as umbrella stands
in the forms of tree trunks. It is believed Walley influenced the creation of these objects. Walley was dissatisfied for financial reasons and had to leave the company.

Walley purchased an old pottery that was formerly the
Wachusett Pottery in West Sterling, Massachusetts. He
unearthed his own red clay from a hillside behind the pottery then designed, modeled, fired, and sold his pottery by
himself. He truly epitomized the Arts and Crafts
Movement's ideals in his statement:

*"I am just a potter trying to make art pottery as
it should be made ... Make one man's ideas, one
man's work. Everything [is] made by hand. To me
there is more true art in a brick made and burnt by
one man than there is in the best piece of molded
pottery ever made. What I feel we want is to be true
to ourselves and let the art come out."*

Walley exhibited his pottery at the Boston Society of
Arts and Crafts in 1907 and was given the title of Master
Craftsman between 1908 and 1918.

Walley's ambitions and talents were not utilized solely
for the purpose of a successful pottery operation. In 1913,
he taught pottery making to patients at Worcester State
Hospital in a craft program entitled "Industrial Therapeu-
tics." This form of therapy was created by the founder of
Marblehead Pottery, Dr. Herbert J. Hall.

Walley's pottery was the clear embodiment of the arts
and crafts spirit. His glazes reflected the beauty of the fall
leaves around his studio in Sterling, Massachusetts. His
most intriguing works incorporate small elf-like figures
sitting on handles or incorporated into the body of the ves-

Walley Pottery fish vase with high glaze, $7,500. (*Collection of Rod Mckenzie*)

sel. Since Walley was a one-man operation, his works are relatively scarce, especially outside the New England area. Walley was certainly familiar with the work of Hugh Robertson and seemed to be able to master any glaze or form. He may have been inspired by the forms published in *Keramic Studio* or other potteries that exhibited at the Boston Society of Arts and Crafts. This could explain some of the architectural forms that had little to do with his natural surroundings. Walley's fine glazes on classical forms represent some of the finest works of the art pottery movement in America.

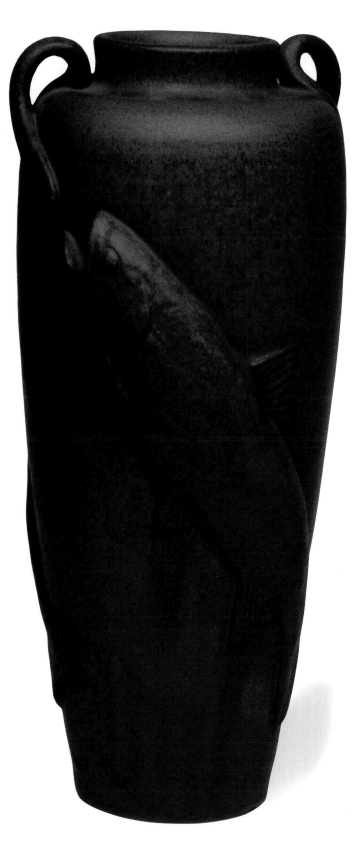

Walley Pottery fish vase with matte glaze, $10,000. (*Skinner*)

Walley Pottery vase with leaf pattern under a
matte glaze, $2,000. (*Collection of Rod Mckenzie*)

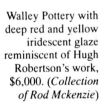

Walley Pottery with
deep red and yellow
iridescent glaze
reminiscent of Hugh
Robertson's work,
$6,000. (*Collection
of Rod Mckenzie*)

Walley Pottery tile depicting a swimming
turtle, $1,200. (*Collection of Rod Mckenzie*)

Walley Pottery vase with reticulated leaf pattern under a high glaze, $10,000. (*Collection of Rod Mckenzie*)

Walley Pottery cabinet vase, $450.

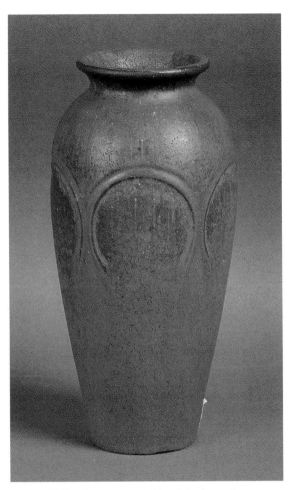

Walley Pottery vase with the yellow, rust, and brown colors of the fall leaves in New England, $5,000. (*Collection of Rod Mckenzie*)

Walley Pottery vase with subtle decoration, $1,500. (*Collection of Rod Mckenzie*)

Walley Pottery vase with frothy highlights on shoulder, $3,000. (*Collection of Rod Mckenzie*)

Walley Pottery vase with incised design, $1,000.

Walley Pottery vase with incised fern design, $2,000.

Walley Pottery candlestick, $300.

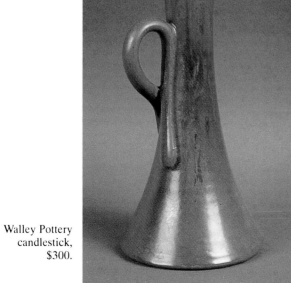

Unusual Walley Pottery wallpocket, $2,000. (*Collection of Rod Mckenzie*)

133

Walley Pottery vase with double gourd form, $2,500. (*Skinner*)

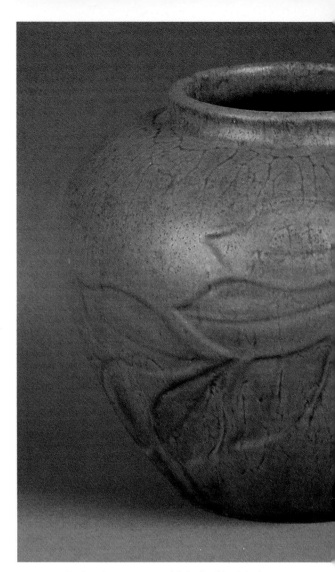

Walley Pottery vase with incised leaf design, $3,000. (*Collection of Rod Mckenzie*)

Walley Pottery vases, $200 each.

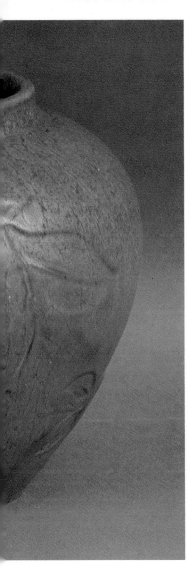

Walley Pottery vase, $2,500.
(*Collection of Rod Mckenzie*)

Walley Pottery vase with
bronze-like glaze, $3,000.
(*Collection of Rod Mckenzie*)

Walley Pottery vase, $1,500.
(*Collection of Rod Mckenzie*)

Walley Pottery vase with blue/gray high glaze, $2,000.

Walley Pottery
cabinet vase, $400.
(*Skinner*)

Walley Pottery vase, $2,000. (*Skinner*)

Walley Pottery vase similar to Saturday Evening Girls glaze, $800.

Walley Pottery vase with ruffled rim, $500.

Walley Pottery leaf form vase, $1,500.

Three Walley Pottery cabinet vases, $200 each.

Walley Pottery vase, $400.

Walley Pottery vase, $400.

138

Walley Pottery covered
jar, $400. (*Skinner*)

Walley Pottery mug, $150.

Walley Pottery vases, $500 each.

Walley Pottery vase, $400.

Walley Pottery devil or elf face pitcher,
$1,500. (*Collection of Rod Mckenzie*)

Side of pitcher.

Walley Pottery
vase, $300.

140

Walley Pottery vase with black high glaze, $500.

Walley Pottery covered jar, $400.

Walley Pottery hair receiver, $700.
(*Collection of Rod Mckenzie*)

Walley Pottery
vase, $350.

141

Walley Pottery vase
with leaf design, $400.

Walley Pottery vase with glaze similar
to Hugh Robertson's work, $500.

Walley Pottery vase with unusual form,
$1,500. (*Collection of Rod Mckenzie*)

142

Walley Pottery miniature lamps, $200 each.

Walley Pottery stove tile, $400.

Walley Pottery vase, $1,200.

Walley Pottery
bowl and cabinet
vase, $200 each.

Walley Pottery
vase, $1,500.
(*Collection of
Rod Mckenzie*)

144

Walley Pottery cabinet vases, $200 each.

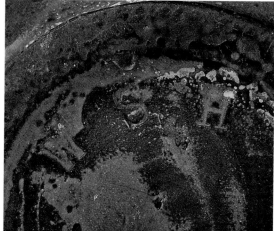

Walley Pottery mark of WSH,
for Worcester State Hospital, as
found on the bottom of a vase.

Walley Pottery vase made at Worcester State Hospital, Worcester,
Massachusetts, $1,200. (*Collection of Rod Mckenzie*)

145

Walley Pottery vase with leaf design, $1,500. (*Skinner*)

Walley Pottery vase, $2,000. (*Collection of Rod Mckenzie*)

Walley Pottery devil or elf pitcher with red inset glass eyes, $1,200.

Walley Pottery cabinet vase and mug, $200 each.

Walley Pottery vase with unusual handles, $1,500. (*Collection of Anthony Leite*)

Walley Pottery cabinet vase, $400. (*Collection of Anthony Leite*)

Walley Pottery vase, $400. (*Collection of Anthony Leite*)

Walley Pottery vase with leaf design, $1,200. (*Collection of Anthony Leite*)

Walley Pottery vase, $1,200. (*Collection of Anthony Leite*)

Walley Pottery vase, $300. (*Collection of Anthony Leite*)

Walley Pottery vase, $400. (*Collection of Anthony Leite*)

Walley Pottery vase with incised design, $1,000. (*Collection of Anthony Leite*)

Walley Pottery cabinet vase, $300. (*Collection of Anthony Leite*)

Walley Pottery vase, $500. (*Collection of Anthony Leite*)

Walley Pottery candlestick, $400. (*Collection of Anthony Leite*)

150

Unusual Walley Pottery wallpocket,
$1,500. (*Collection of Anthony Leite*)

Walley Pottery vase, $3,000. (*Collection of Anthony Leite*)

151

Walley Pottery vase, $3,000. (*Collection of Anthony Leite*)

Walley Pottery vase, $2,500. (*Collection of Anthony Leite*)

Walley Pottery vase, $1,500.
(*Collection of Anthony Leite*)

Walley Pottery vase,
$3,000. (*Collection
of Anthony Leite*)

Walley Pottery vase, $2,000. (*Collection of Anthony Leite*)

Walley Pottery vase, $1,500. (*Collection of Anthony Leite*)

Walley Pottery vase,
$300. (*Collection of
Anthony Leite*)

Walley Pottery vase with unusual modern design, $500. (*Collection of Anthony Leite*)

Walley Pottery vase, $1,000. (*Collection of Anthony Leite*)

Walley Pottery candlestick, $400. (*Collection of Anthony Leite*)

155

Walley Pottery
cabinet vase,
$400.

Walley Pottery leaf-form
vase, $2,000. (*JMW Gallery*)

Walley Pottery vase, $1,500.
(*Collection of Anthony Leite*)

Walley Pottery lamp,
$500. (*JMW Gallery*)

Walley Pottery vase,
$1,000. (*JMW Gallery*)

Walley Pottery vase, $1,500. (*JMW Gallery*)

Walley Pottery candlesticks, $450. (*JMW Gallery*)

Walley Pottery vase, $1,500. (*JMW Gallery*)

Walley Pottery flower holder, $500. (*JMW Gallery*)

Walley Pottery candlestick, $200. (*JMW Gallery*)

Chapter 9

MARBLEHEAD POTTERY
(1904-1936)

Marblehead Pottery vase with panther design, $15,000-plus. (*Skinner*)

Marblehead Pottery was the creation of the wonderfully talented mind of Herbert J. Hall, MD.

Dr. Hall was the first person to introduce the concept of work therapy. People suffering from physical ailments and nervous conditions were given work to exercise their body and mind. Various things were produced such as wooden boxes from driftwood, picture frames, copper items, and linens. The workspace was a large old converted barn next to the Devereaux mansion, which was built in 1856. The workspace became known as the Handcraft Shops.

One summer, Alfred Baggs, a student from Alfred University, needed work. Alfred University was considered the best school for the study of ceramics in the United States. His professor,

Marblehead Pottery mark as found on the bottom of a vase.

Charles Binns, wrote to Dr. Hall recommending Alfred for work. At the time, the Handcraft Shops were producing primarily utilitarian pottery. By 1908, the pottery was making 200 vessels a week. The staff in 1909 consisted of Arthur Baggs as director and designer, Arthur Irwin Hennessey (designer), Miss Maude Milner (designer), E.D. (Hannah) Tutt (decorator), John Swallow (English potter in charge of throwing), and E.J. Lewis who took care of the kiln.

In 1908, a *Keramic Studio* review of the National Society of Craftsmen Exhibition praised the work of the pottery:

"The best new work in ceramics was undoubtedly that sent by the Handicraft Shop of Marblehead, Mass., of which

Marblehead Pottery vase with conventionalized flowers, $6,000. (*Skinner*)

Marblehead Pottery floral vase, $4,000. (*JMW Gallery*)

Mr. Arthur E. Baggs is guiding spirit. The forms are simple and good, the designs also are restrained and in good taste. The colors are soft and subdued, yet varied, with a pleasant matt texture. The designs are in flat glazes with incised outlines—showing good control of the medium—an altogether noteworthy exhibit."

The pottery quickly outgrew its roots. Production could not keep up with demand and Arthur Baggs purchased the pottery from Dr. Hall in 1915. Under his guidance, the pottery would receive many awards over the years including the J. Ogden Armour Prize at the annual exhibition of applied arts at the Art Institute of Chicago, the highest award by the Boston Society of Arts and Crafts in 1925 and first prize in both the Robineau Memorial Exhibition at the Syracuse Museum of Fine Arts in 1933 and the National Ceramic Exhibition in 1938. Towards the end of his career, Baggs spent more time teaching at the School of Design and Liberal Arts in New York and the Cleveland School of Art. By 1936, the Great Depression took its toll on sales and the pottery was forced to close.

The pottery produced at Marblehead is subtle and soothing. The forms are sensual in their presence with gently tapering lines. Glazes included soft, plain colors including blue, green, brown, and yellow invoking images of local gardens and the sea. Decorated items have simple, conventionalized floral sprays or animals. Specially decorated wares by Arthur Baggs display an almost Japanese woodblock print look to them, probably influenced by Arthur Wesley Dow in nearby Ipswich, Massachusetts. Dow utilized the rhythm and harmony of Japanese art and created a design theory taught in schools throughout the country.

Marblehead Pottery is highly collected among art pottery lovers. Recently some items came to market that descended through the family of Dr. Hall including a double-tile frieze, *Poplars with Reflections*, that sold for $21,850.

Marblehead Pottery vase with beautiful berry design, $4,000. (*JMW Gallery*)

Marblehead Pottery tobacco-brown vase with incised floral design. Incised designs are believed to be earlier than simply painted designs, $1,500. (*Skinner*)

Marblehead Pottery vase, $1,500. (*JMW Gallery*)

Rare Marblehead Pottery vase with flat-painted,
conventionalized floral motif, $8,000. (*Skinner*)

Marblehead Pottery vase with incised design, $1,800. (*JMW Gallery*)

Rare Marblehead Pottery vase with incised,
conventionalized floral motif, $10,000. (*Skinner*)

Opposite page:
Marblehead Pottery vase with
severely conventionalized and incised
tree design, $7,000. (*JMW Gallery*)

Unusual Marblehead Pottery vase
with striated, iridescent glaze, $6,000.

Marblehead Pottery vase, $3,500. (*Skinner*)

Marblehead Pottery vase with incised design on what is
the classic Marblehead blue glaze, $3,000. (*Skinner*)

Marblehead Pottery vases, $2,500-4,500. (*Skinner*)

Marblehead Pottery vases, $4,000-8,000. (*Skinner*)

165

Rare Marblehead Pottery vase
with experimental glaze by
Arthur Baggs, $10,000. (*Skinner*)

Marblehead Pottery bowl, $800. (*Skinner*)

Marblehead Pottery
bowl, $3,000. (*Skinner*)

Marblehead Pottery tile, *Poplars with Reflection*.
This tile frieze set the world record for Marblehead
at auction, drawing more than $21,000. (*Skinner*)

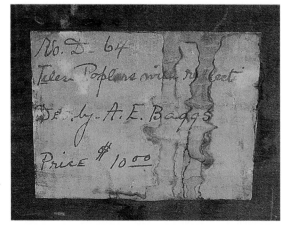

Back of tile.

167

Marblehead Pottery tile, the scene resembles the work of the woodblock print artist Arthur Wesley Dow, $5,000. (*JMW Gallery*)

Marblehead Pottery tile with garden scene reminiscent of the gardens in Marblehead, Massachusetts, $3,000.

Marblehead Pottery tile with flat-painted sailing ship, $900.

Marblehead Pottery tile with raised ship decoration, $750.

Marblehead Pottery bowl, incised
design of sailing ship, $500.

Marblehead Pottery vases, $200, $400, 300. (*JMW Gallery*)

Marblehead Pottery bookends, one of the few
items made with a mold, $750. (*JMW Gallery*)

Marblehead Pottery
vase with deep
green glaze, $1,500.
(*Skinner*)

Marblehead Pottery vase with rare, speckled-
green glaze, $2,000. (*JMW Gallery*)

Marblehead Pottery vase, $1,500. (*JMW Gallery*)

170

Marblehead Pottery vase with lavender glaze, $2,000. (*JMW Gallery*)

Marblehead Pottery vase with subtle tapering form, $1,200. (*Skinner*)

Marblehead wallpocket, $400

Marblehead Pottery cylindrical vase, $800.

171

Marblehead Pottery vase with unusual form, $1,500. (*JMW Gallery*)

Unusual Marblehead Pottery wall pocket, $475.

Marblehead Pottery vases, $300, $200.

Marblehead Pottery vase with a beautiful form, $1,200. (*JMW Gallery*)

Marblehead Pottery vases with classic Marblehead blue glaze, $200, $150, $400.

Marblehead Pottery vase
with speckled yellow
glaze, $1,500. (*Skinner*)

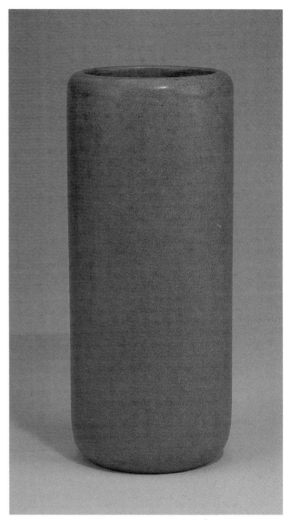

Marblehead Pottery vase, $1,200.

Marblehead Pottery vases,
$400, $300, $350.

174

Marblehead vase, $250

Marblehead Pottery vase, $400.

Marblehead Pottery vase with
rare pink glaze, $700. (*Skinner*)

Marblehead Pottery bowl with lavender glaze, $300.

Marblehead Pottery candlestick, $300. (*Skinner*)

Marblehead Pottery covered box, $1,200. (*JMW Gallery*)

176

Marblehead Pottery mugs, $300 each.

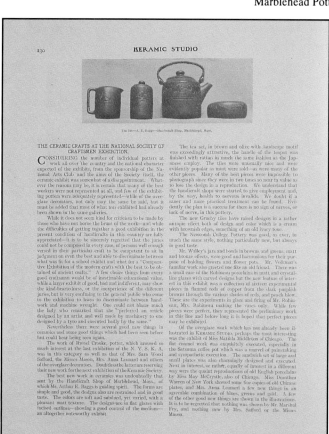

Keramic Studio magazine, 1908, Review of
National Society of Craftsmen Exhibition.

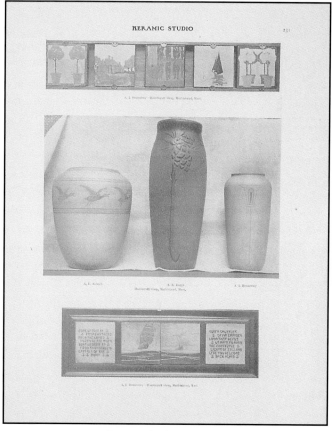

Keramic Studio magazine.

Chapter 10

SATURDAY EVENING GIRLS/PAUL REVERE POTTERY
(1906-1942)

Saturday Evening Girls bowl with interior band decoration, $7,000-plus. (*JMW Gallery*)

Saturday Evening Girls mark as found on the bottom of a plate showing date 5/19 and artist initials.

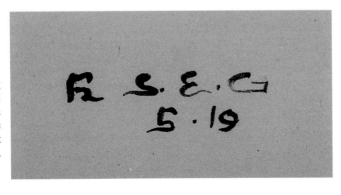

Saturday Evening Girls mark changed to Paul Revere Pottery and used this logo to sign wares.

Saturday Evening Girls brochure.

Edith Guerrier was born in 1870 in New Bedford, Massachusetts. Her mother died while she was only three years old and her father, needing help, left her with various relatives until she finally settled with an aunt and uncle in Concord, Massachusetts. Her aunt and uncle, Walton and Anna Ricketson, were familiar with the mid-nineteenth century literary circles of Concord. Under their influence, she was able to attend the Vermont Methodist Seminary and Female College in Montpelier where she would have come into contact with the writings of John Ruskin.

After graduating, Guerrier enrolled at the Museum School of Boston's Museum of Fine Arts for artist training. Edith Brown was a fellow student who befriended Guerrier. Due to financial difficulties, Guerrier began to work in the day nursery at the North Bennet Street Industrial School. Edith Brown and Guerrier moved in together, beginning a lifelong business and personal relationship.

Guerrier's duties expanded at the North Bennet Street Industrial School to include maintaining the reading room. The clubs were composed of Italian, Jewish, and Irish girls. The reading clubs expanded until the Boston Public Library was forced to open a permanent branch in the North End of Boston.

Helen Osborne Storrow was on the Board of Managers of North Bennet Street School and a member of the Board of Visitors of the Boston Public Library. It was through these activities that Guerrier and Storrow met. Helen and her husband, James Jackson Storrow, Jr., were both supporters of social and educational programs for immigrants. The Storrow's had a successful business and were great supporters of the Boy and Girl Scouts of America. The well known Storrow Drive in Boston was created by Helen after the death of her husband.

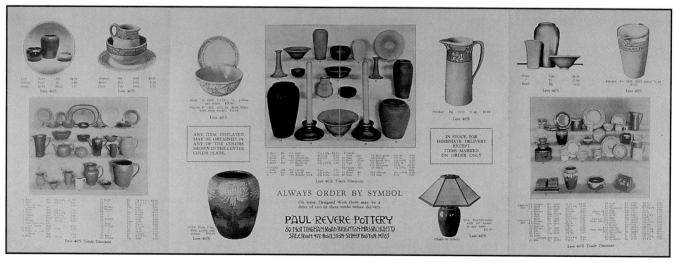

Inside the Saturday Evening Girls brochure. Note that some items
were more than a month's wages for the average worker of the time.

Saturday Evening Girls brochure.

Helen Storrow befriended Edith Guerrier and Edith Brown and when Guerrier's health suffered, Storrow sent both Ediths on a trip to the Swiss Alps to rest. During the trip, Guerrier and Brown discussed ideas for earning extra money for the girls in the Saturday Reading Clubs.

"We spoke of making marmalade, or fruitcake, of hemming napkins and dishtowels, and finally, we spoke of pottery, of the charming peasant ware of Italy, of Holland, of Germany, and now of Switzerland. Since our club girls were almost all of peasant stock, why not start an art pottery and produce American peasant ware?"

Edith Brown was experienced with producing clay. The North Bennet Street Industrial School had a modeling room and kiln which was used to teach pottery classes as early as 1907. With the help of funding from Helen Osborne Storrow, Guerrie and Brown began what would become the Paul Revere Pottery in 1906.

A former chemist of Merrimac Pottery in Newburyport, Massachusetts, was hired and pottery was made in the cellar of Guerrier and Brown's Chestnut Hill Home. The items were signed S.E.G. for Saturday Evening Girls. Helen Storrow was enthusiastic about the pottery and purchased a four-story brick house on Hull Street in the North End to house the pottery and library clubs in 1908. The building was located near the Old North Church where Paul Revere hung his famous lantern, and henceforth the pottery became known as the Paul Revere Pottery.

Edith Brown was a full-time designer for the pottery. At this time, there were approximately fifteen full-time women involved with making pottery. Between 1906 and 1912, the pottery was a commercial venture receiving press in many magazine articles and selling their products through mail order and gift shops. The designs that decorated the pottery were based upon a mixture of Japanese line and Greek architectonic patterns translated through charming children's motifs of pigs, rabbits, turtles, and

Saturday Evening Girls bowl with incised floral decoration, $3,000. (*JMW Gallery*)

Saturday Evening Girls bowl with exterior band decoration, $8,000-plus. (*JMW Gallery*)

Rare Saturday Evening Girls bowl, $15,000-plus. (*Skinner*)

flowers. Edith Brown utilized the teachings of Arthur Wesley Dow. He taught the Japanese notion of line in which an object is recognized by its contour and color is nothing more than the surface that fills in the contour.

By 1915, the pottery would move to Nottingham Road in Brighton, Massachusetts. The company was officially incorporated on February 4, 1916 as Paul Revere Pottery with Helen Storrow, Edith Guerrier, and Edith Brown as directors, each having a one-third share of ownership. The pottery was never fully a financial success. By the late 1920s, it was close to financial ruin and pottery was donated to the Society for the Preservation of New England

Antiquities in 1926. The company continued in vain. In 1932 Edith Brown passed away and finally, in 1942, production was discontinued.

Saturday Evening Girls pottery represents some of the best aspects of the Arts and Crafts Movement. Its designs based upon Japanese and Greek aesthetic principles conveyed through children's motifs of animals and striking floral displays are enchanting. Its social reform activities to help young women find work and financial freedom represent the movement's best ideals. As more people become aware of the role of these women, the demand for Saturday Evening Girls pottery will increase dramatically.

Saturday Evening Girls
bowl with conventionalized
floral decoration, $2,000.
(*JMW Gallery*)

Saturday Evening Girls bowls, $200 each.

Saturday Evening Girls bowl depicting Paul Revere's ride, $4,000. (*Skinner*)

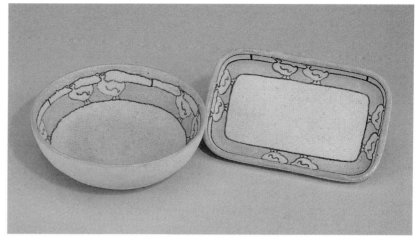

Saturday Evening Girls bowl and tray with duck pattern, $200 each.

Early Saturday Evening Girls bowl, $500.

Saturday Evening Girls plate, $1,200. (*JMW Gallery*)

**Saturday Evening
Girls plate with
Greek design, $300.
(*JMW Gallery*)**

Saturday Evening Girls plate with border decoration, $1,000. (*JMW Gallery*)

Saturday Evening Girls plates with Greek design, $200 each. (*Skinner*)

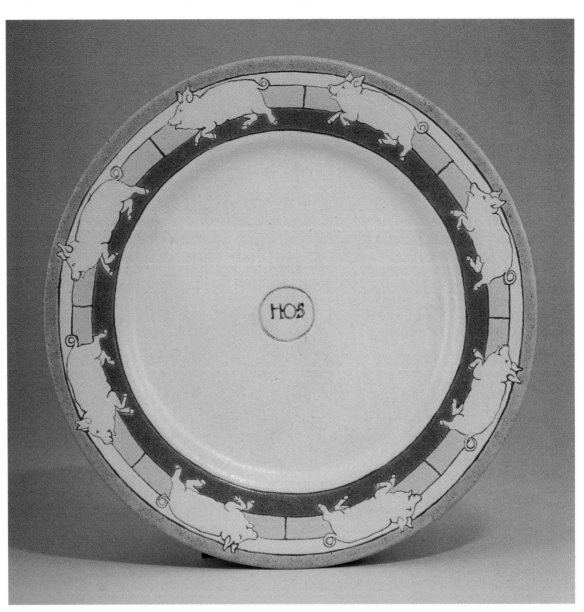

Saturday Evening Girls plate with trees, $400. (*JMW Gallery*)

Saturday Evening Girls plate, $400. (*Skinner*)

Saturday Evening Girls plate with
reticulated handles, $450. (*JMW Gallery*)

Saturday Evening Girls plate, $400. (*JMW Gallery*)

Opposite page top:
Saturday Evening Girls plate, initials could
be special ordered, this series of pig pattern
plates are believed to have been ordered by
Helen Osborne Storrow, $2,000.

Opposite page bottom:
Saturday Evening Girls plates, $400 each.

Saturday Evening Girls trivet, $500. (*JMW Gallery*)

Saturday Evening Girls tile, $750. (*Skinner*)

Saturday Evening Girls tile of Boston Common, $1,200. (*JMW Gallery*)

188

Saturday Evening Girls partial luncheon set, $400.

Saturday Evening Girls partial dinner service, $3,000. (*Skinner*)

189

Saturday Evening Girls partial tea set, $500.

Saturday Evening Girls salts and butter pads, $40 each.

Saturday Evening Girls bowl and cup and saucer, $300 each.

Saturday Evening
Girls cup and saucer,
$600. (*JMW Gallery*)

191

Saturday Evening Girls cup and saucer, $600. (*Skinner*)

Saturday Evening Girls cup and saucer, $750. (*Skinner*)

Saturday Evening Girls pitcher, $750. (*Skinner*)

Rare Saturday Evening Girls swan pattern—
a graceful design and form, $1,500. (*Skinner*)

193

Saturday Evening Girls pitcher, $700.

Saturday Evening Girls miniature cups, $250 each. (*JMW Gallery*)

Saturday Evening Girls water set, $750.

Saturday Evening Girls candlesticks, $600. (*Skinner*)

Saturday Evening
Girls honey pot,
$2,000. (*Skinner*)

Unusual Saturday Evening Girls jar, $4,000.

Saturday Evening Girls vase, $1,500. (*Skinner*)

Saturday Evening Girls vase, $3,000. (*Skinner*)

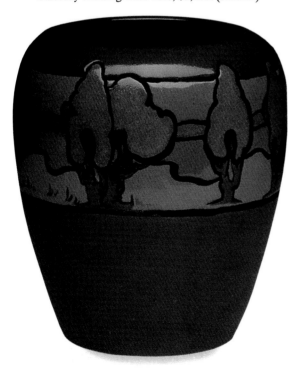

Saturday Evening Girls vase, $300.

197

Saturday Evening Girls vase, $5,000. (*Skinner*)

Saturday Evening Girls pottery, pitchers, and plates $300-500 each, large bowl $1,000.

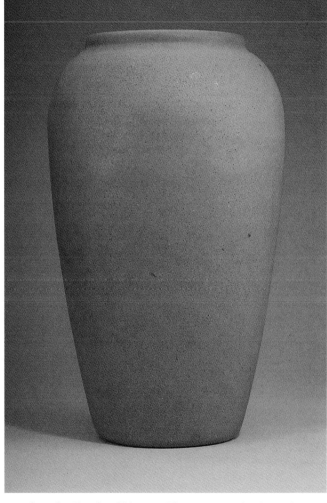

Saturday Evening Girls vase. These vases tend to be made later in the '20s and '30s and show less innovation and rely mainly on glazes for decoration, $800. (*JMW Gallery*)

Saturday Evening Girls vase with dripping glaze, $400.

DORCHESTER POTTERY

(1928-1979)

Dorchester Pottery swirling pattern dinnerware, $50-300 each.

Although Dorchester Pottery is not truly part of the Arts and Crafts Movement, the pottery began to produce items in harmony with the Arts and Crafts Movement aesthetic before other art pottery companies such as Dedham Pottery closed. The Dorchester Pottery Company was founded in 1895 by George Henderson. In the early years, the pottery concentrated on making commercial stoneware items including the Henderson Footwarmer which accounted for twenty-nine percent of their sales. By 1910, Henderson obtained a permit to construct a new kiln. The kiln was built by specialists from Germany and it measured twenty-two feet in diameter, ten-and-a-half feet high.

It allowed for three freight cars of pottery to be fired at one time. By 1925, five or six potters were turning out hundreds of pieces each day, producing bean pots, casseroles, jugs, crocks, footwarmers, and mixing bowls along with commercial ware.

In 1928, Charles Henderson died and the family decided to introduce a decorative stoneware. The Great Depression caused the commercial stoneware business to suffer and Ethel Hill Henderson, a former industrial art teacher and fabric designer, began to decorate her stoneware with motifs of old New England. The designs included pine cones, blueberries, strawberries, the Sacred Cod, and Greek scrolls in blue-and-white decoration.

The items were created on a wheel and hand decorated. Ethel's brother, Charles Allen Hill, joined the company, adding new mixing color techniques from his career as a chemistry teacher. Other decorators included Joseph McCune, Phil Spear, Ronald Brakee, Robert Trotter, Jackie Burn Callder, Rhoda Ricci, and Knesseth Denison.

Items can be found with the signatures of "Charles Hill" and "Nando Ricci" along with "Dorchester Pottery." Ethel Hill Henderson died in 1971 and subsequent pieces are signed "I.M.E.H.H." (In Memorial Ethel Hill Henderson). The company closed in 1979 after a fire.

The pottery reflects the charm of New England and many special order items were made for presidential elections, space missions and alike. The pottery was hand thrown on a wheel and hand decorated and certainly inspired by its forerunners in the art pottery movement like Dedham Pottery. It is an excellent choice for the beginning collector who is interested in New England Art Pottery.

Dorchester Pottery mark as found on the bottom of a plate.

Dorchester Pottery pine cone-pattern dinnerware, $50-300 each. (*JMW Gallery*)

Dorchester Pottery floral patterns, $200 each.

Dorchester Pottery floral items, $30 each.

202

Dorchester Pottery plate, $150.

Dorchester Pottery plate, $100.

Dorchester Pottery plate—scenes are always more desirable, $350.

Dorchester Pottery plate, $125.

Unusual Dorchester Pottery plate, $100.

Dorchester Pottery pitcher and plate, $400 each.

Dorchester Pottery plates, $400, $300, $250. (*JMW Gallery*)

Dorchester Pottery pitcher, $175; plates, $75 each; creamer, $30.

Dorchester Pottery covered witch sugar $250,
floral pitcher $250, pine cone pitcher $200.

Dorchester Pottery cups $50 each.

Dorchester Pottery star dish $75, plate $75, bowl $100.

Dorchester Pottery commemorative dish for the Apollo XI mission, $250.

Detail of back of
Apollo XI plate.

BIBLIOGRAPHY

Alsop-Robineau, Adelaide. *Keramic Studio*, Syracuse, New York.

Cavallini, William C. "Low's Art Tiles," *New England Tool Collectors Association Scrapbook*, No.14, pg.1, Fall 1992.

Clark, Robert Judson. *The Arts and Crafts Movement in America 1876-1916*, Princeton University Press, 1972.

Eidelberg, Martin. *From Our Native Clay*, New York, The American Ceramics Arts Society, Turn of the Century Editions, 1987.

Evans, Paul. *Art Pottery of the United States*, New York, Feingold & Lewis Publishing Co., 1974.

Grueby Pottery: A New England Arts and Crafts Venture, Hood Museum of Art, Dartmouth College, 1994.

Hawes, M.D., Lloyd E. *The Dedham Pottery and the Earlier Robertson's Chelsea Potteries*, Dedham Historical Society, 1968.

Hercher, Gail Pike. "Marblehead Pottery," *Marblehead Magazine*, Fall 1980.

Johnson, Pamela. *The Journal of Decorative & Propaganda Arts*, Wolfson Foundation of Decorative and Propaganda Arts, 1994.

Keen, Kirsten Hoving. *American Art Pottery*, Delaware Art Museum, Falcon Press, 1978.

Kovel, Ralph & Terry. *Kovel's American Art Pottery*, New York, Crown Publishers, 1993.

McGrath, Vincent F. "Marblehead Pottery," *Sextant: Journal of Salem State College*, Vol. VI, No.2, 1996.

Meech, Julia & Weisberg, Gabriel. *Japonisme Comes to America*, New York, Abrams, 1990.

Meyer, Marilee Boyd. *Inspiring Reform: Boston's Arts and Crafts Movement*, Davis Museum and Cultural Center, 1997.

Montgomery, Susan J. *The Ceramics of William H. Grueby*, New Jersey, Arts & Crafts Quarterly Press, 1993.

Morris, Barbara. *Liberty Design*, New Jersey, Chartwell Books Inc., 1989.

Pappas, Joan & Kendall, A. Harold. *Hampshire Pottery: Manufactured by J.S. Taft &Company*, Vermont, 1971.

Perry, Barbara. *American Ceramics: The Collection of Everson Museum of Art*, New York, Rizzoli, 1989.

A Portfolio of Pottery: Hampshire Ware, 1871.

Robertson, J. Milton. *Dedham Pottery Catalog*, 1938.

Ulehla, Karen Evans. *The Society of Arts and Crafts, Boston: Exhibition Record 1897-1927*, Trustees of the Public Library of the City of Boston, 1981.

Updike, D.B. *Dedham Pottery Formerly Known as Chelsea Pottery U.S.: A Short History*, Boston, The Merrymount Press.

A Village Potter: William J. Walley, Fitchburg Art Museum, 1992

Watkinson, Raymond. *Pre-Raphaelite Art & Design*, New York, 1970.

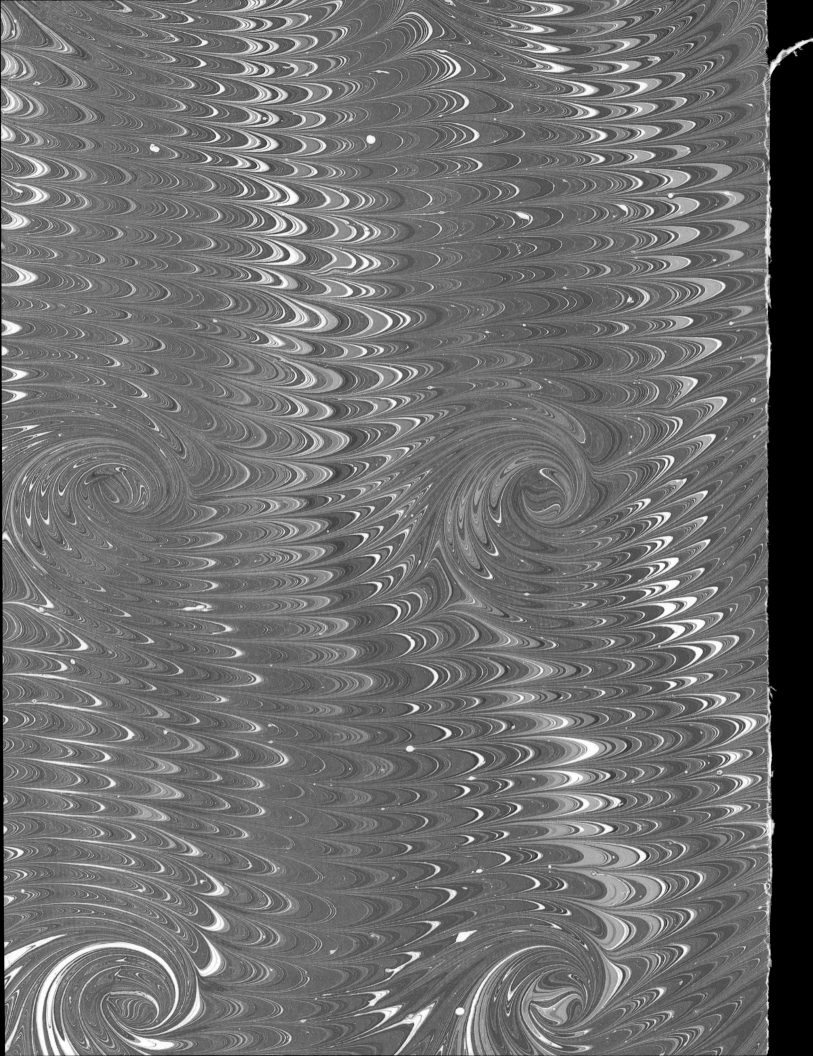